What Is Tao
-
the Seasons

什么是道

-

四季

Dao in Life
生命之道

www.daoinlife.com

Copyright © 2023
Dao in Life
All rights reserved.

www.daoinlife.com

Dedication

To Rosie, who reminds me every day of the beauty and wonder of life.

献给Rosie，她每天都让我想起生命的美丽和奇迹

Introduction

介绍

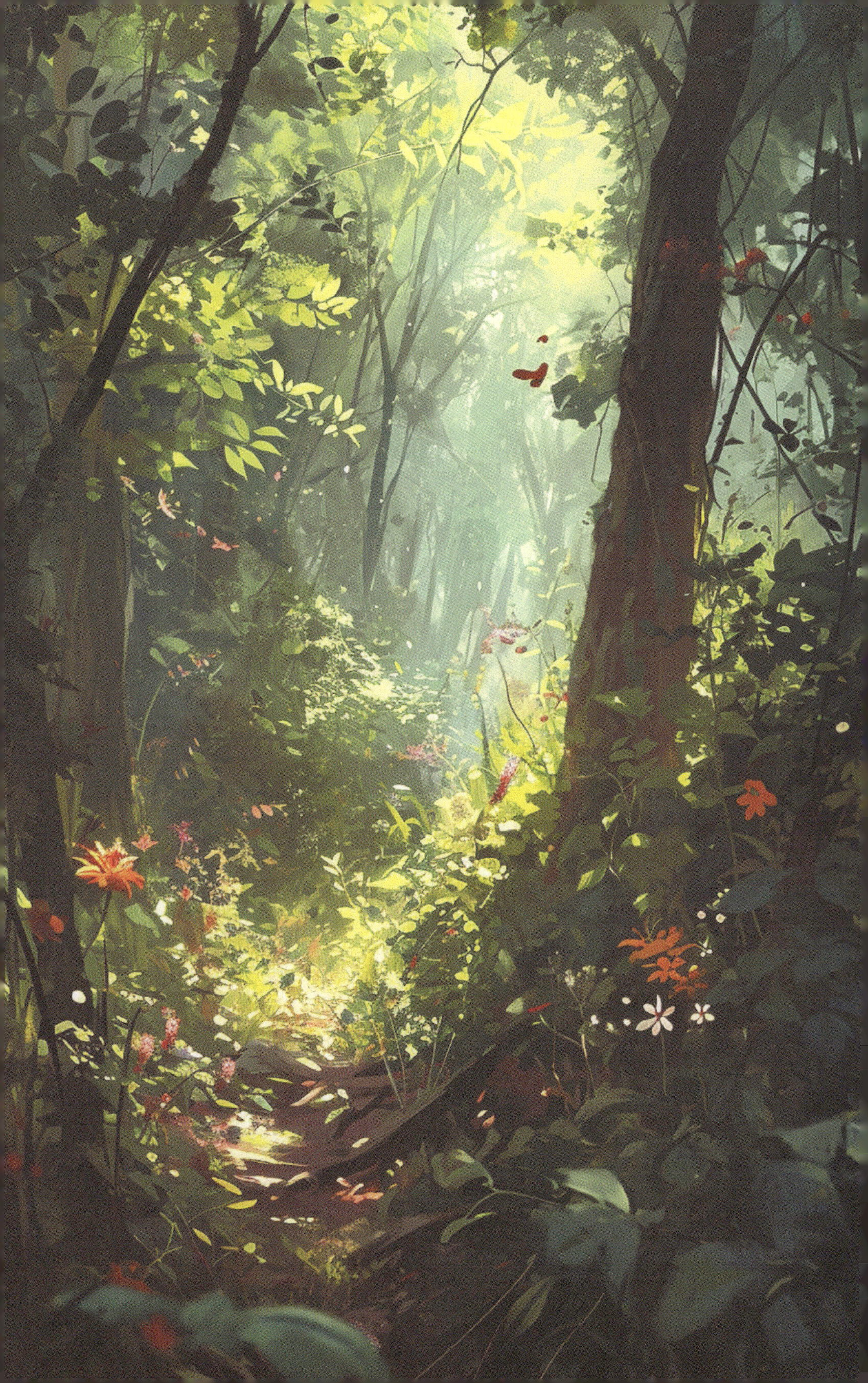

In the heart of a mystical forest,
在神秘森林的中心,

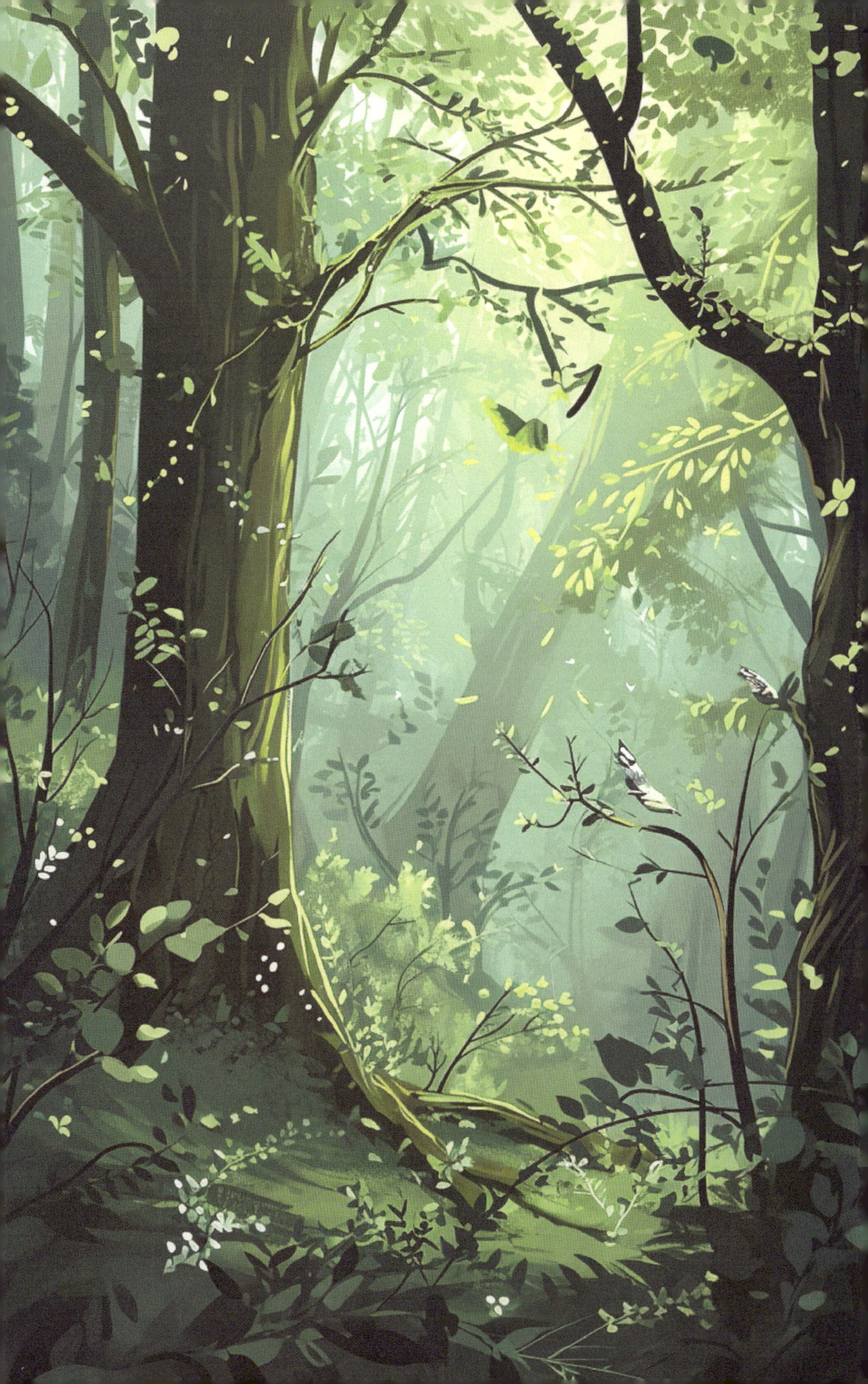

where every leaf whispered ancient secrets and every breeze carried stories of old,
每一片叶子都在低语着古老的秘密，每一阵微风都承载着古老的故事，

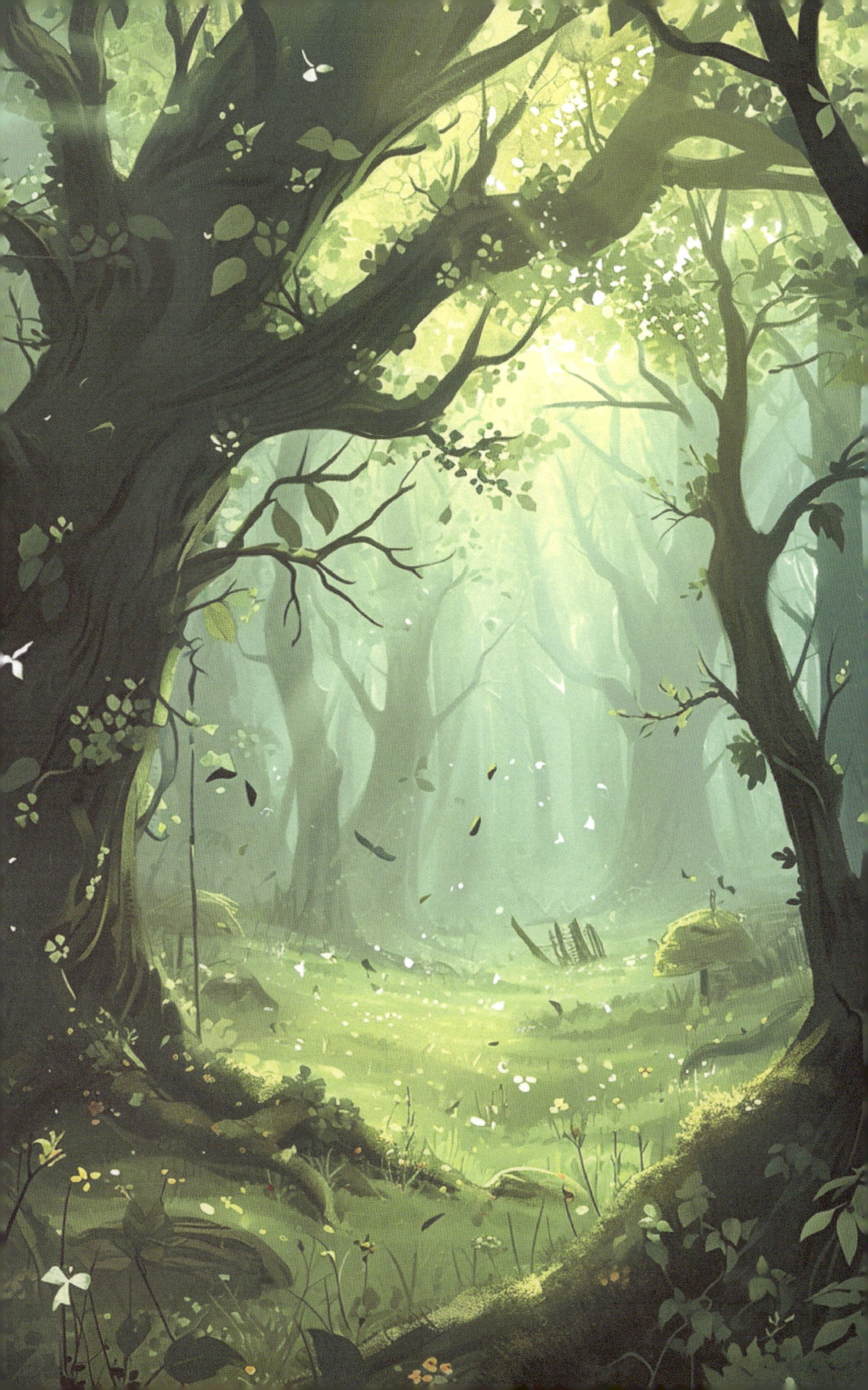

there lived a wise old panda named Master Ping.
那里住着一只智慧的老熊猫，名叫平师傅。

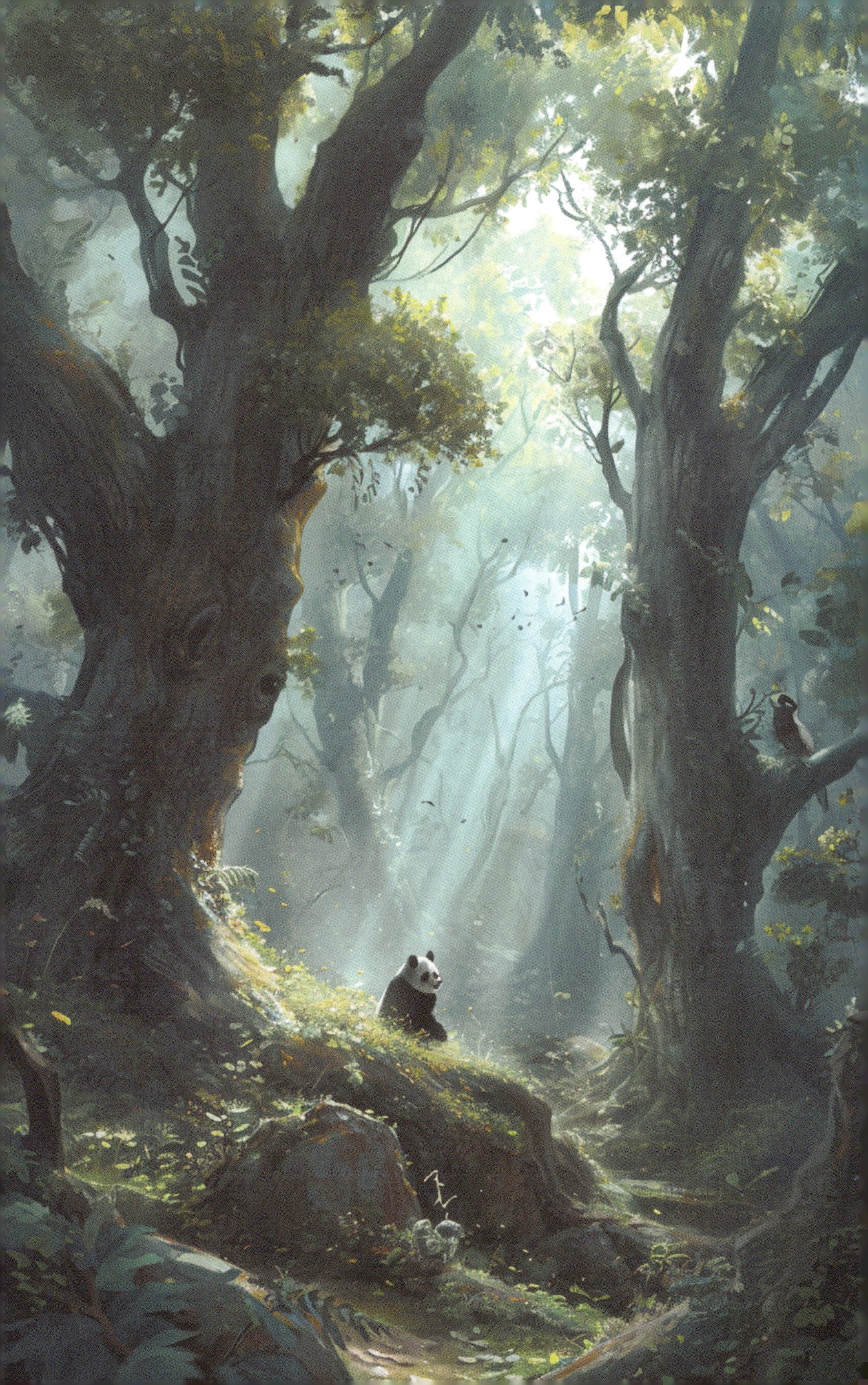

Master Ping was not just any ordinary panda;
平师傅不是普通的熊猫;

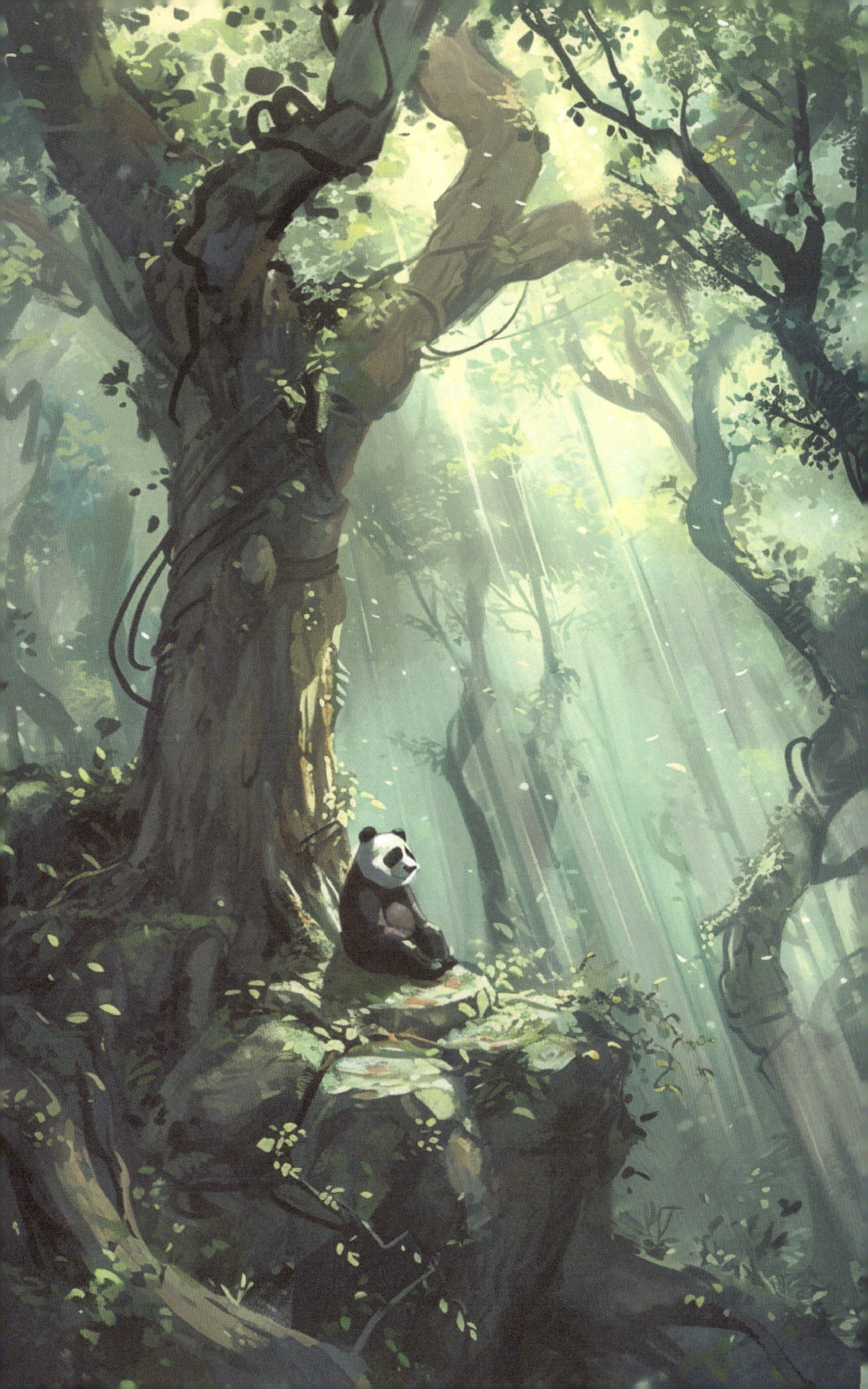

he was the keeper of the forest's wisdom and the guardian of its mysteries.
他是森林智慧的守护者，也是森林奥秘的监护人。

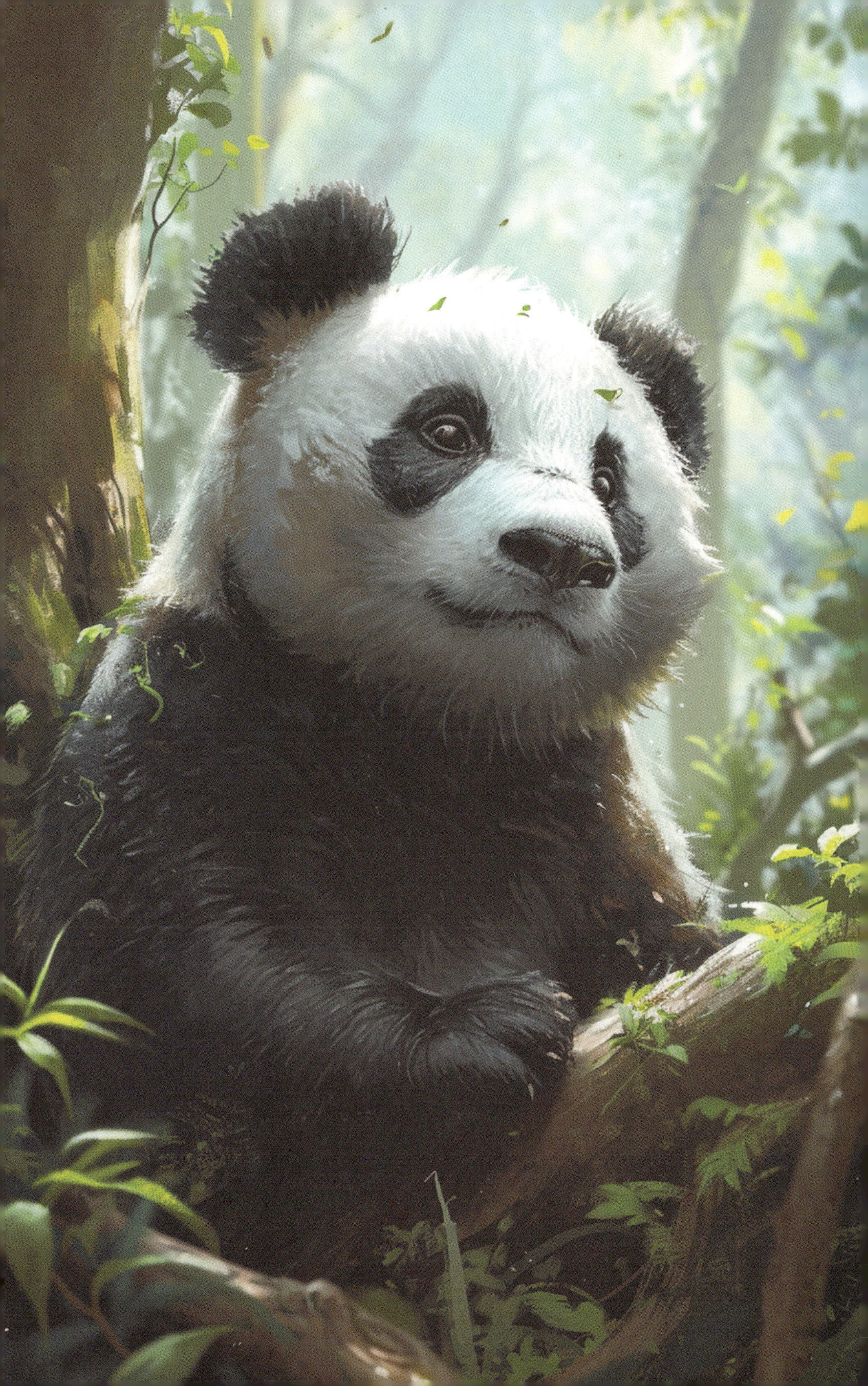

Among his many teachings,
在他的众多教学中，

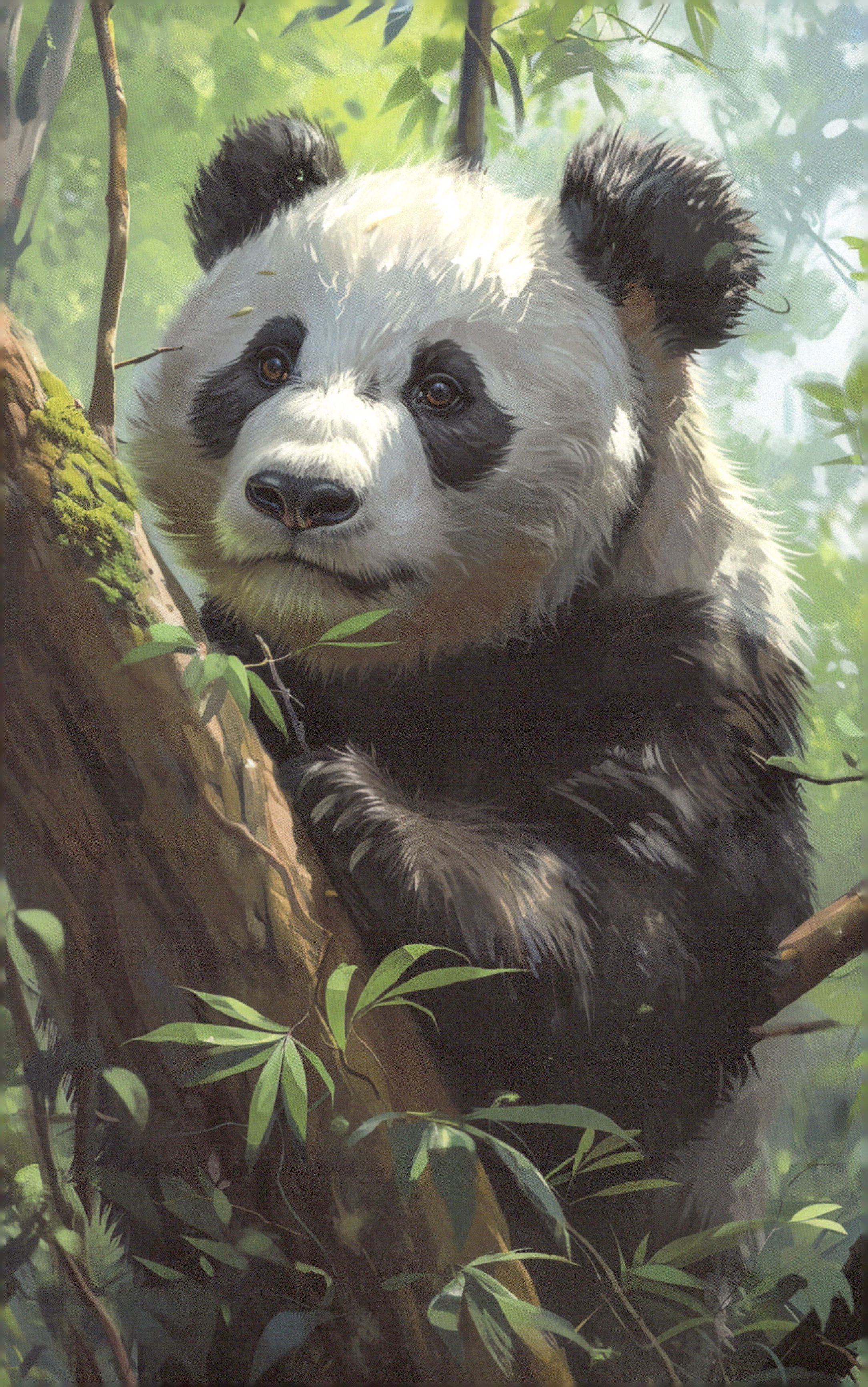

the most profound was the concept of Tao,
最深刻的是道的概念,

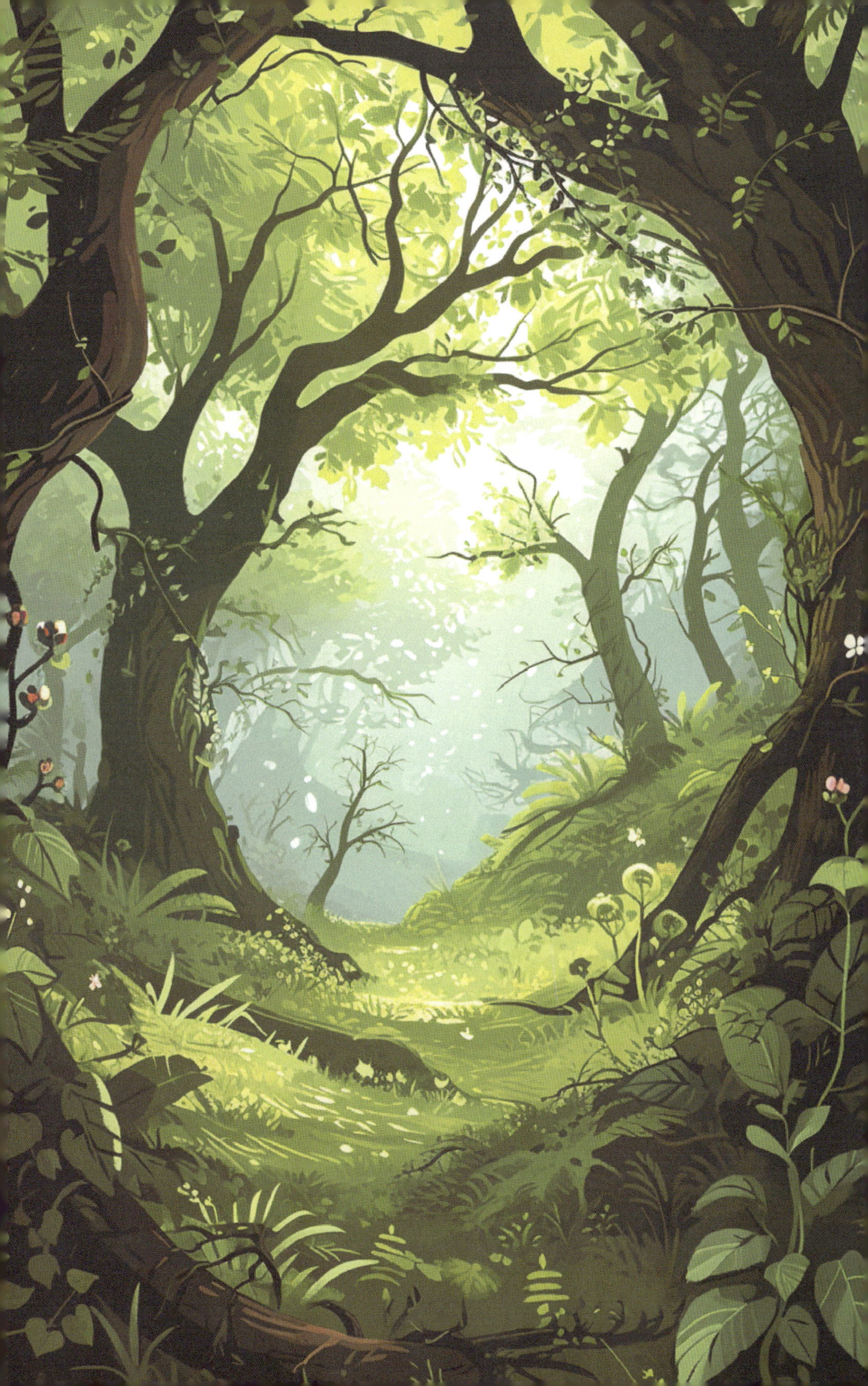

the driving force of life that bound everything in the universe.
绑定宇宙万物的生命驱动力。

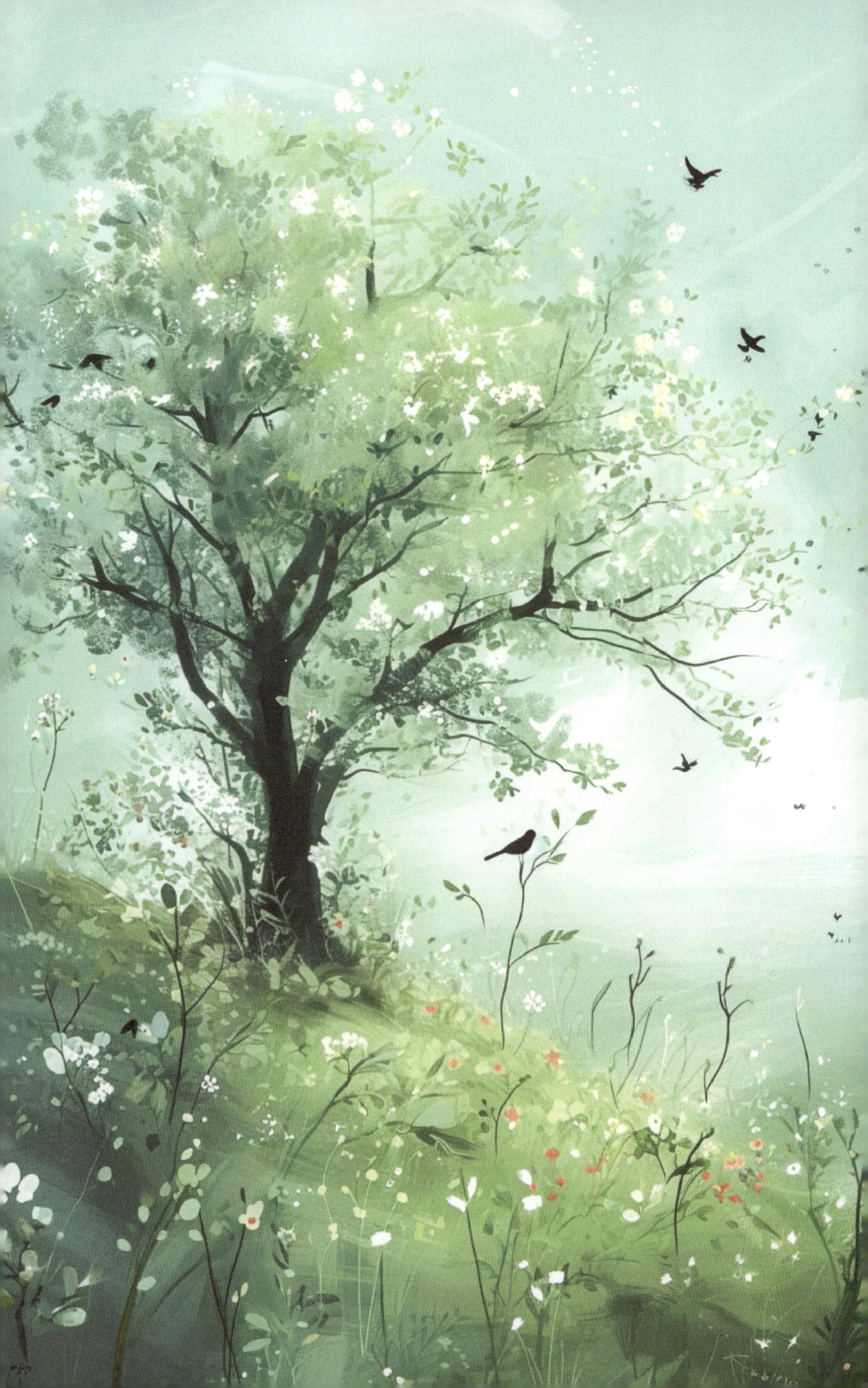

Chapter 1

-

The Spring of Beginnings

第一章

-

春生

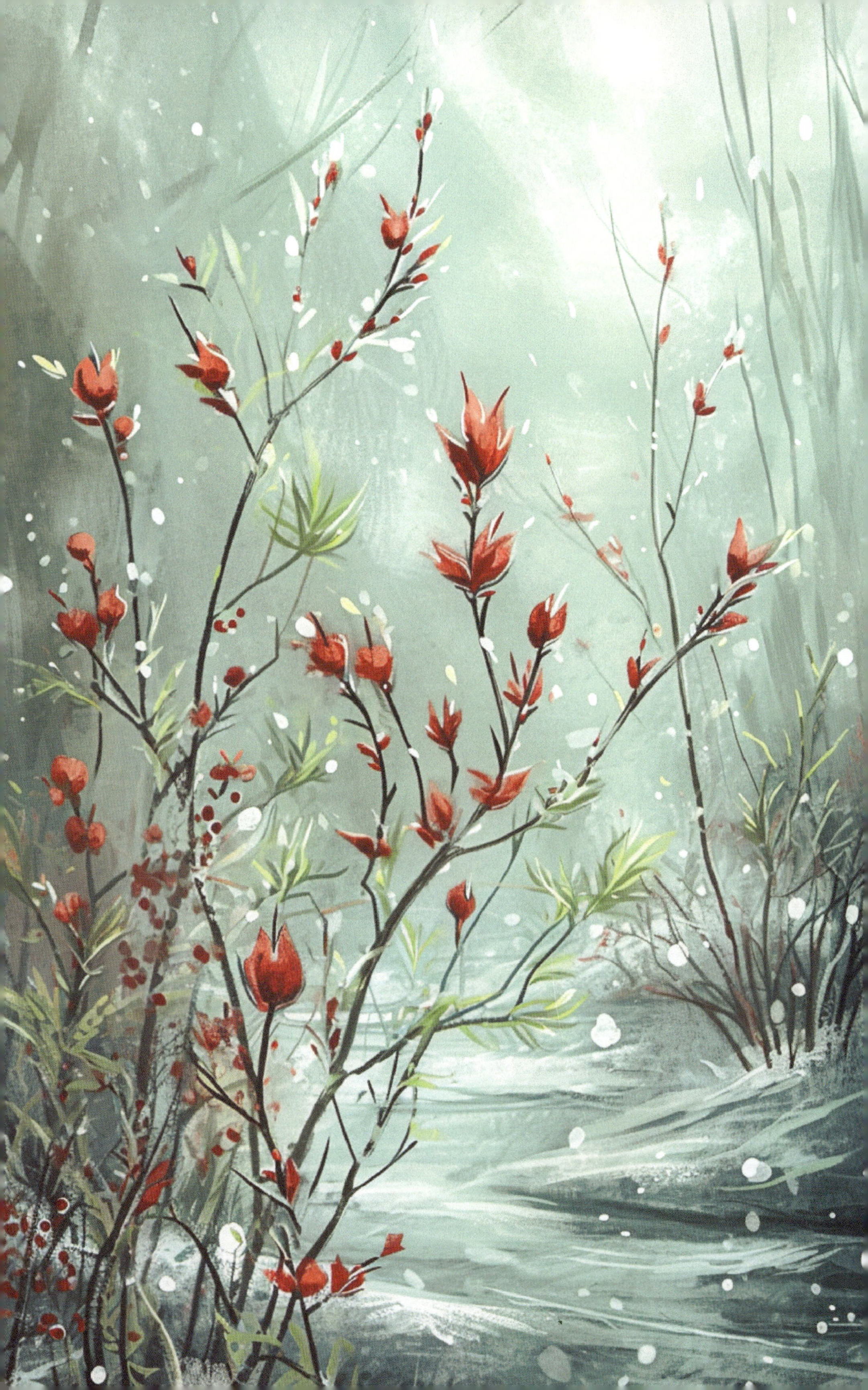

As the winter snow melted and the first buds of spring appeared,
随着冬天的积雪融化,春天的第一缕花蕾出现,

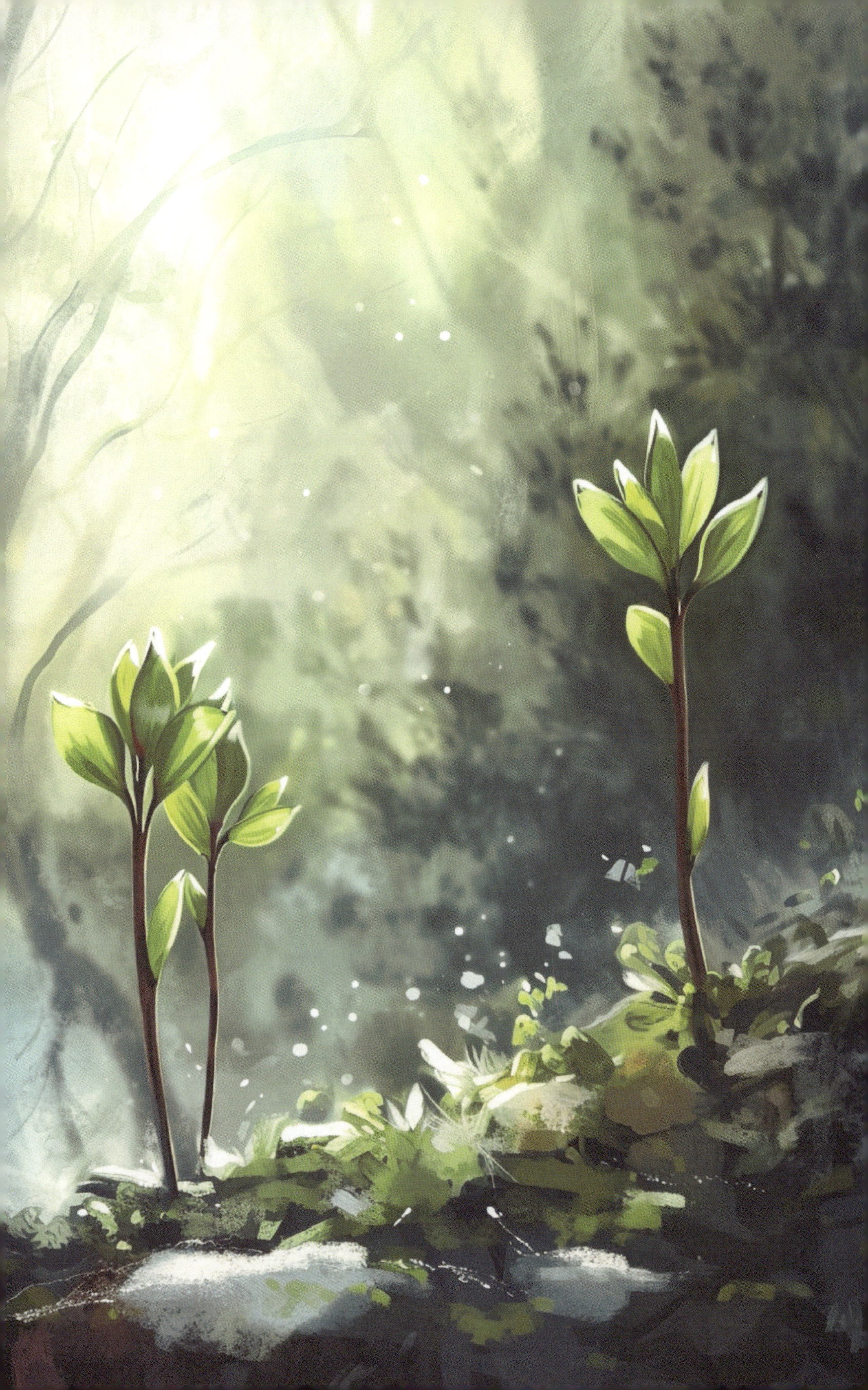

Master Ping gathered the young animals of the forest to share the wonders of Tao.
平师傅召集了森林里的小动物们来分享道的奇妙。

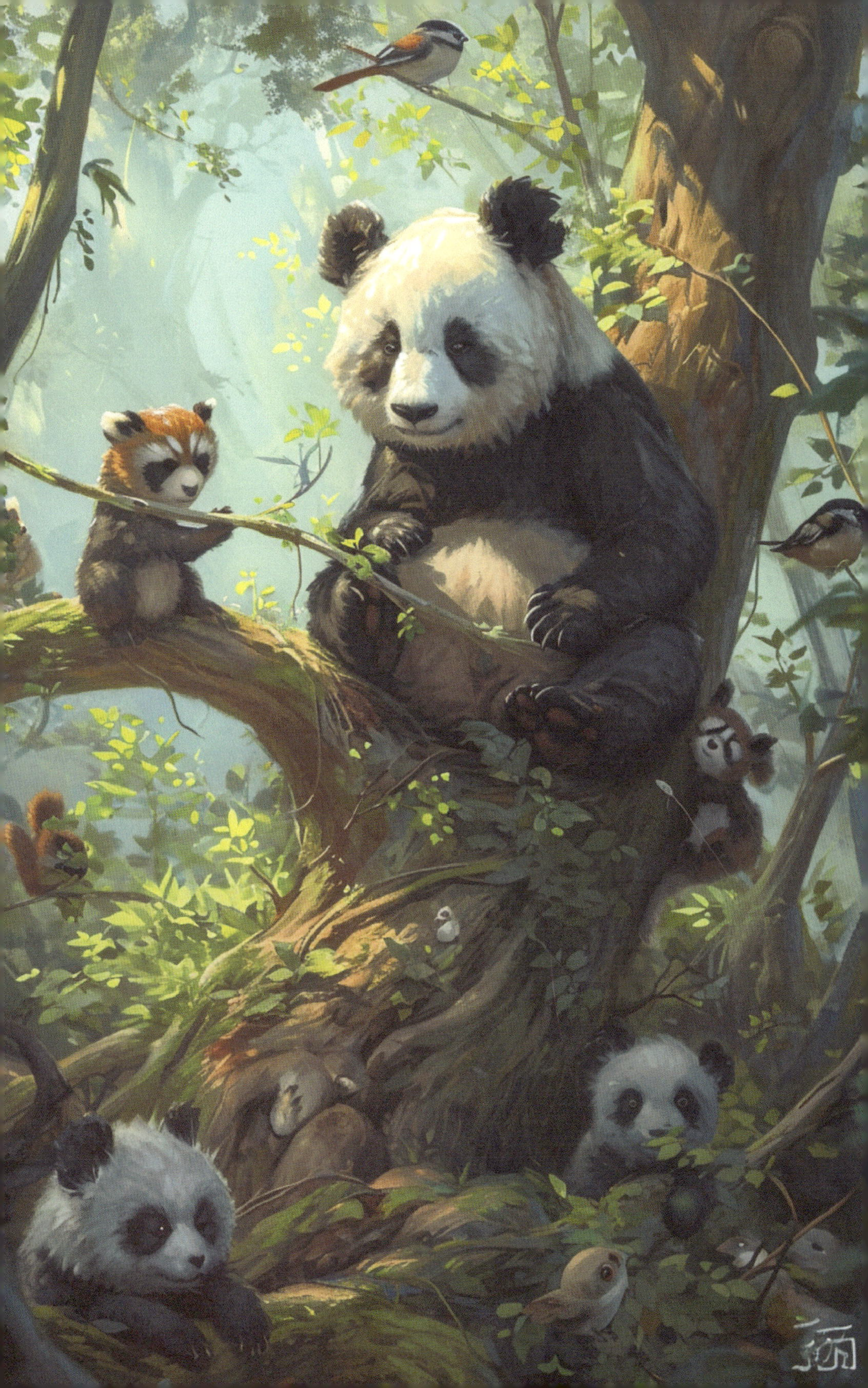

"In spring, everything begins to grow," he explained.
"春天，一切都开始生长，"他解释道。

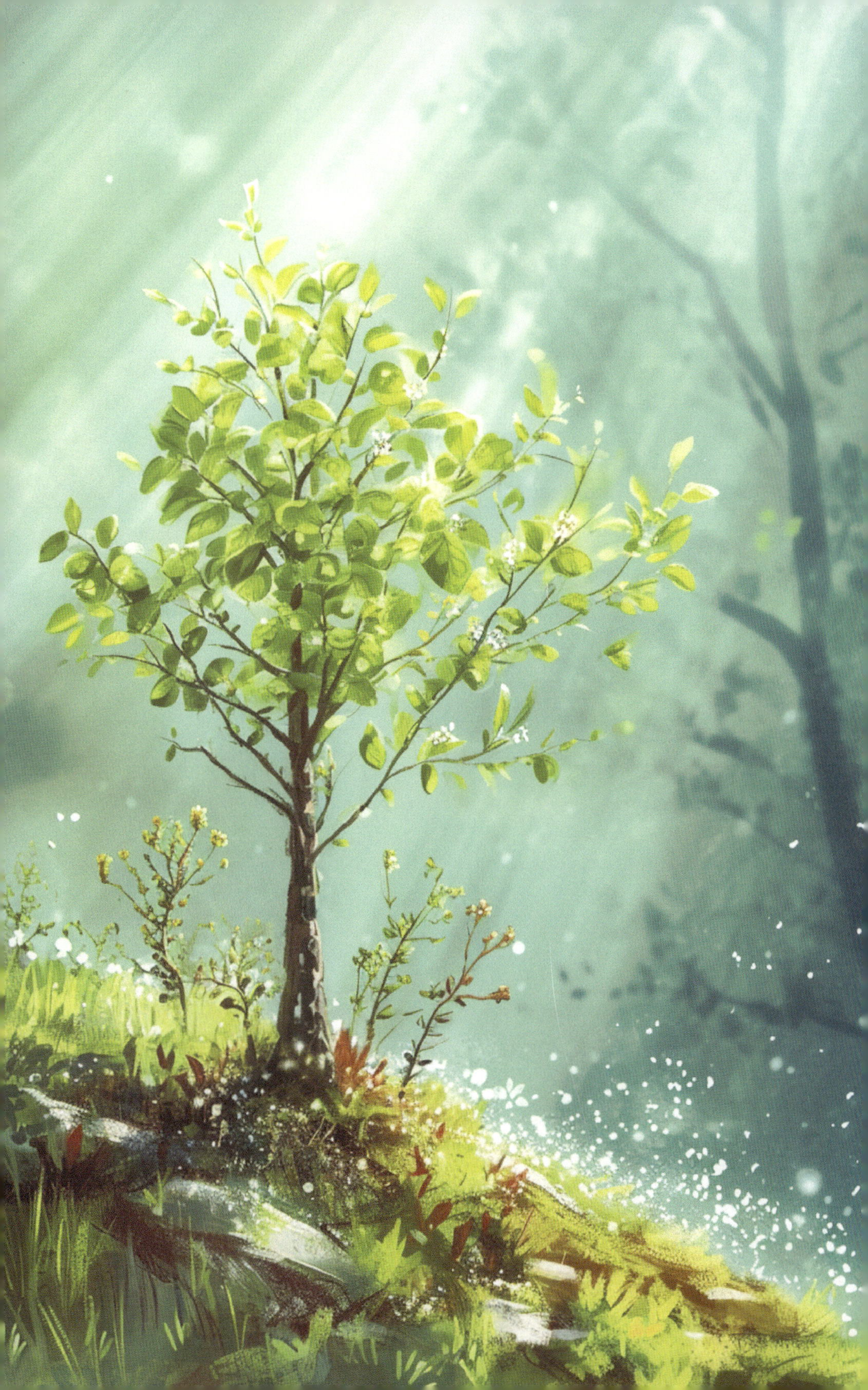

"This is the time of new beginnings,
"这是新开始的时刻,

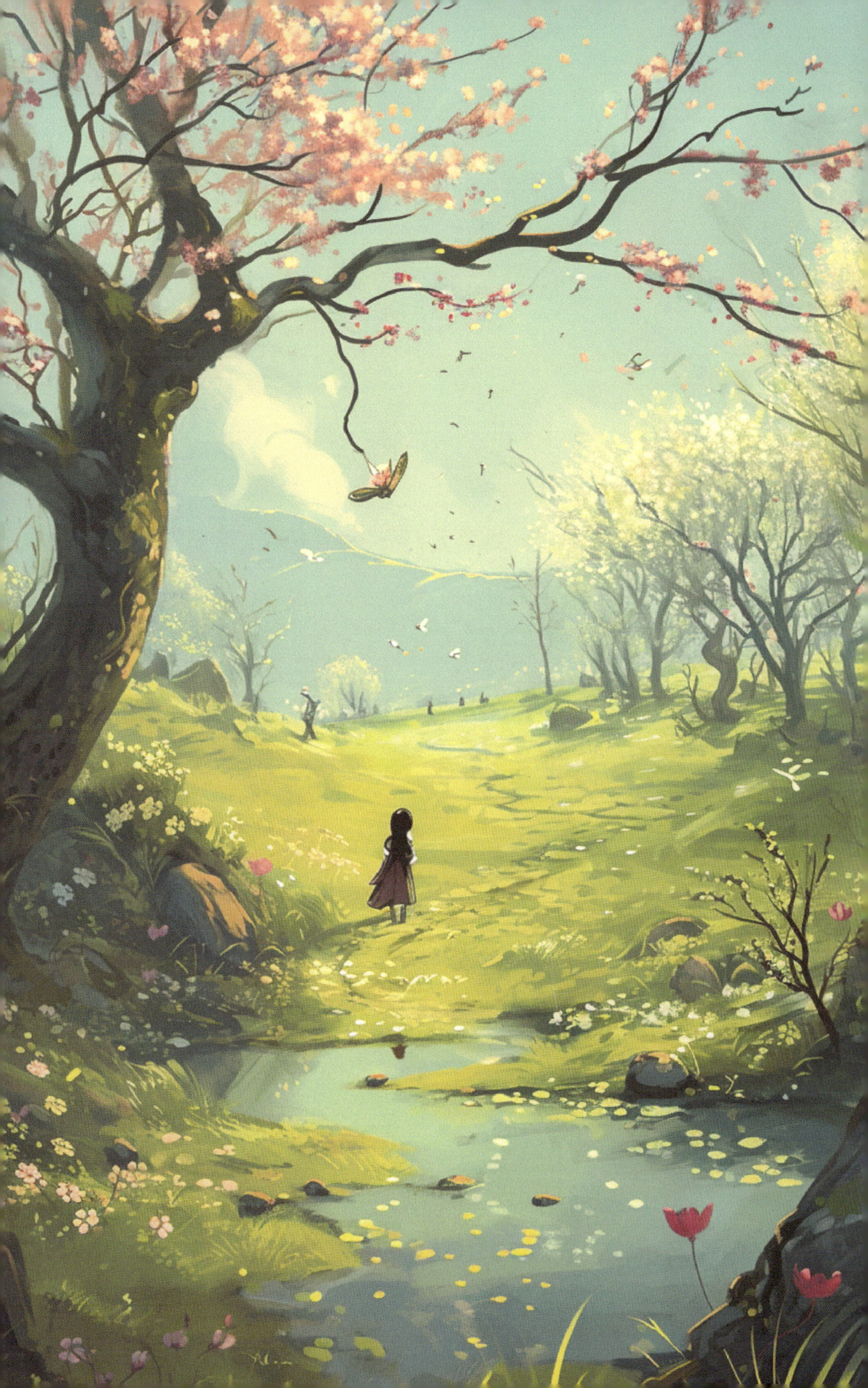

a time when life awakens from its slumber.
生命从沉睡中苏醒的时刻

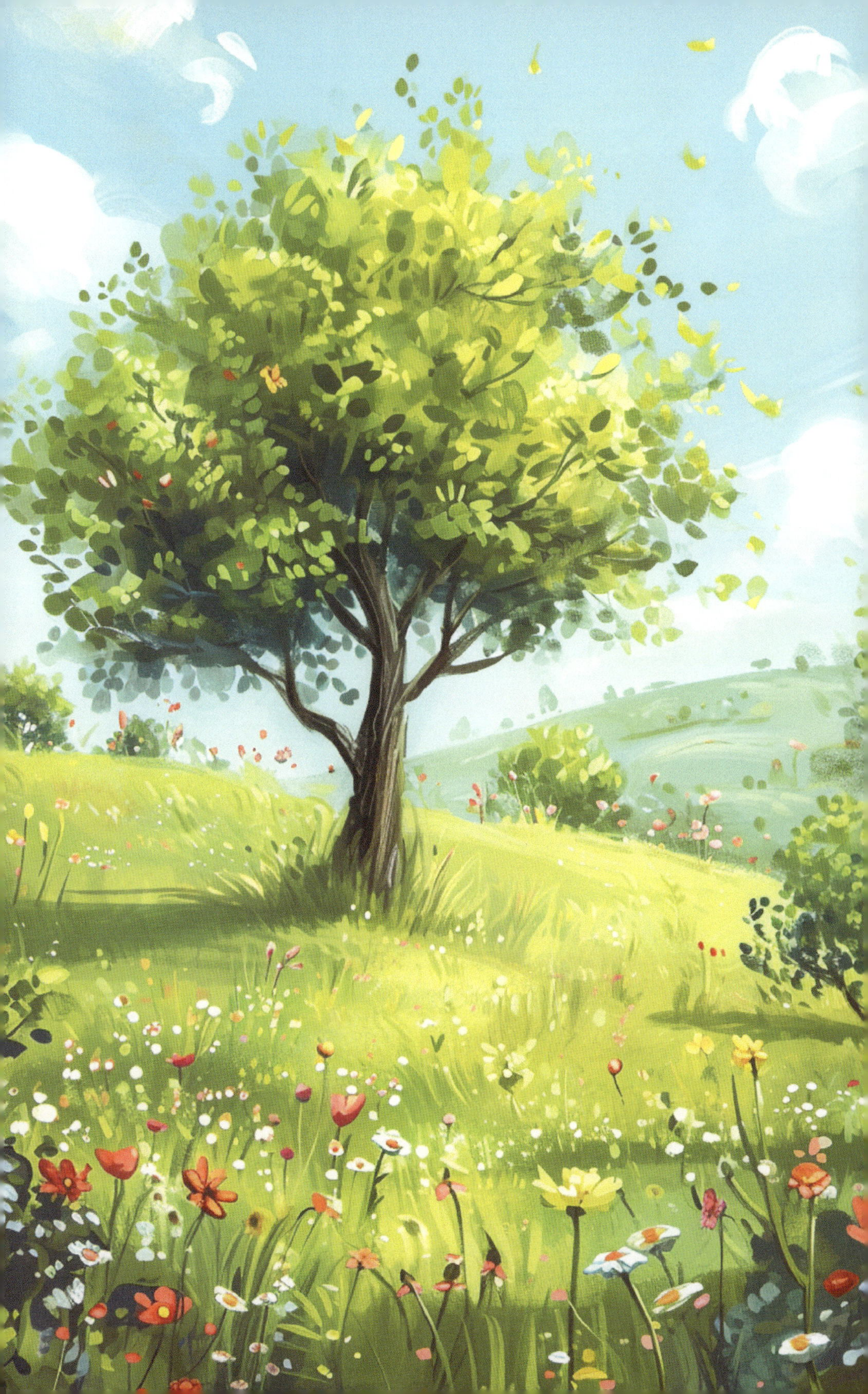

Just like the young birds reaching for the sky,
就像幼鸟飞向天空一样，

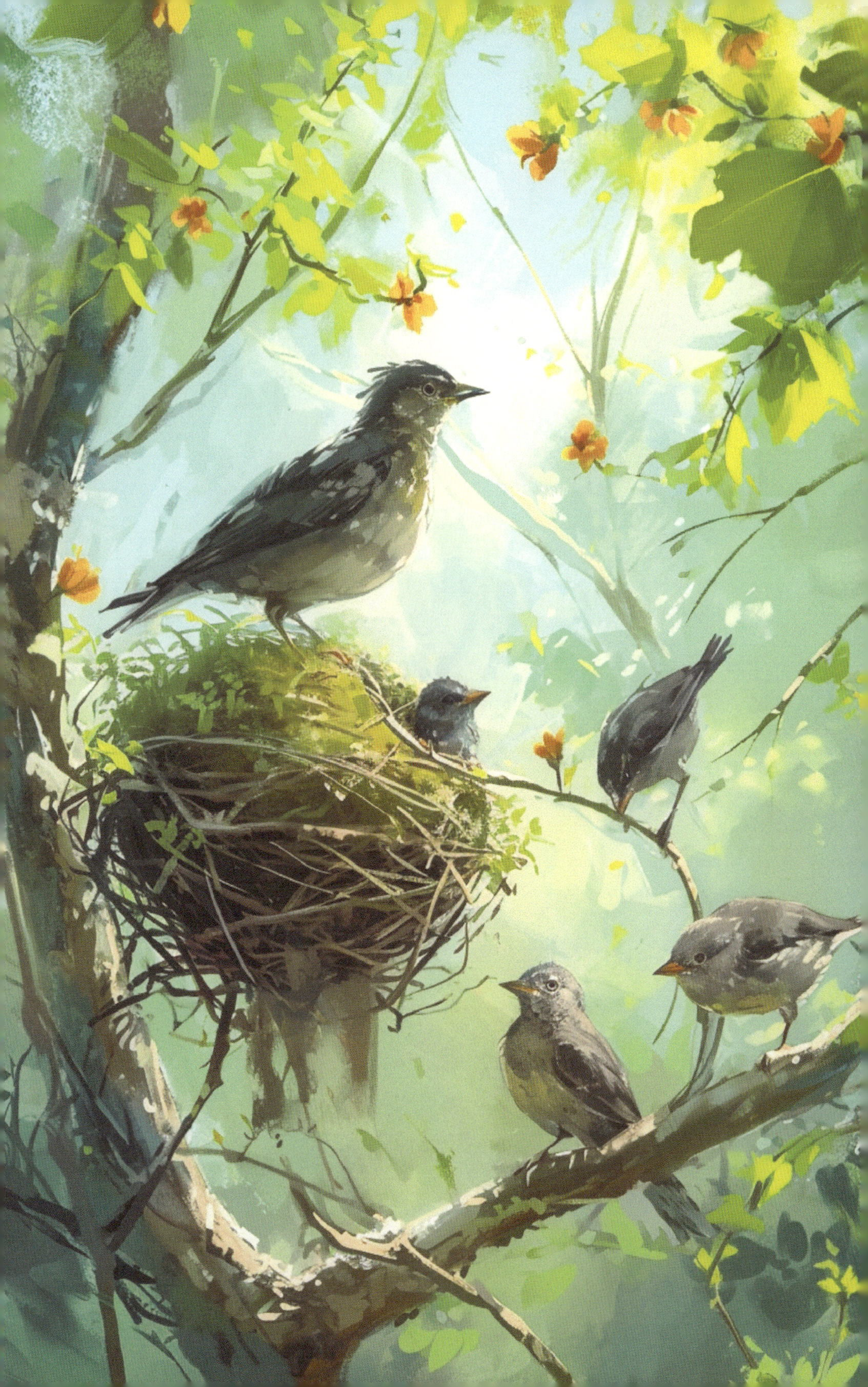

Tao encourages us to grow and explore."
道鼓励我们成长和探索。

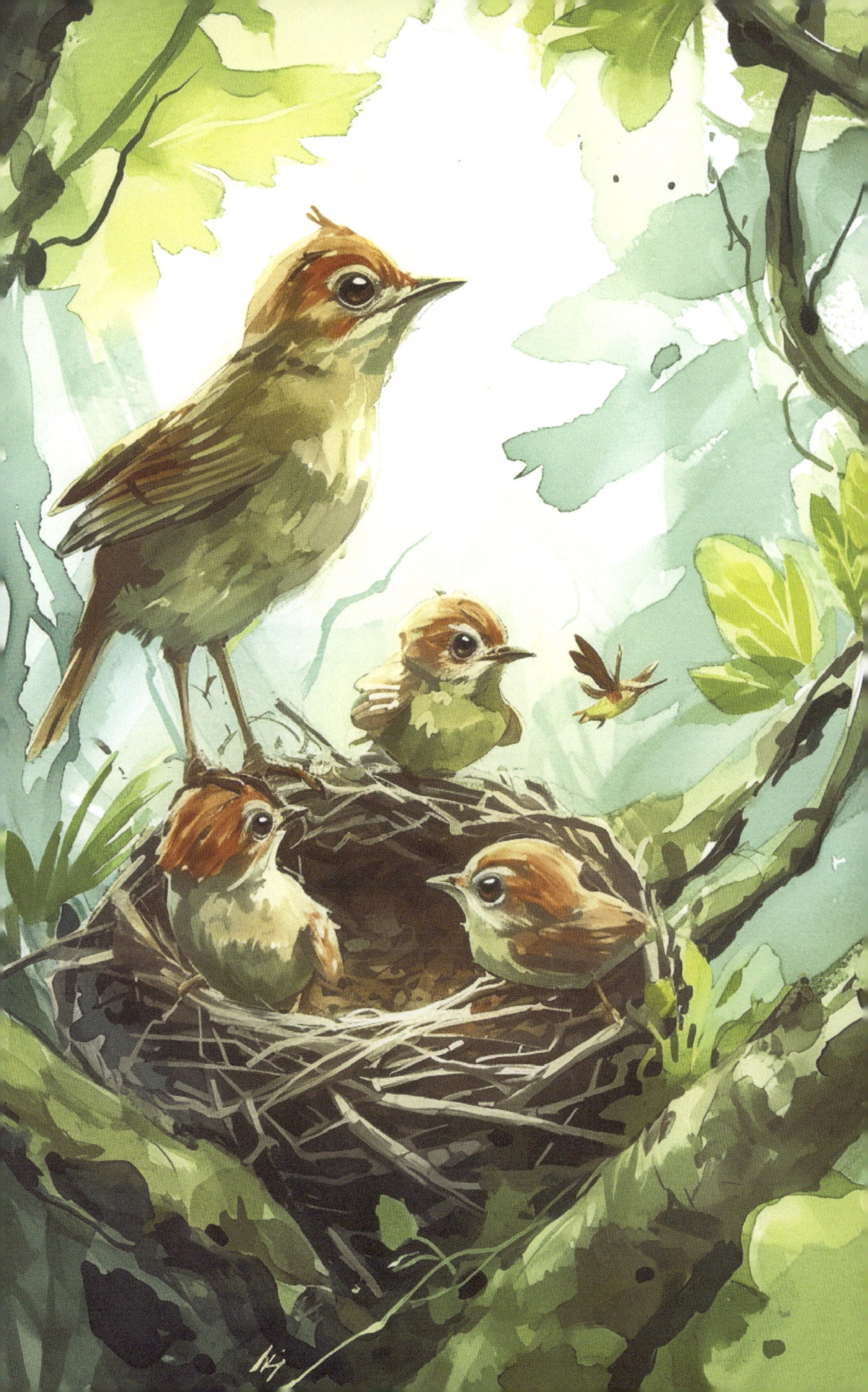

Little Bao, a curious rabbit, hopped excitedly.
小宝，一只好奇的兔子，兴奋地跳了起来。

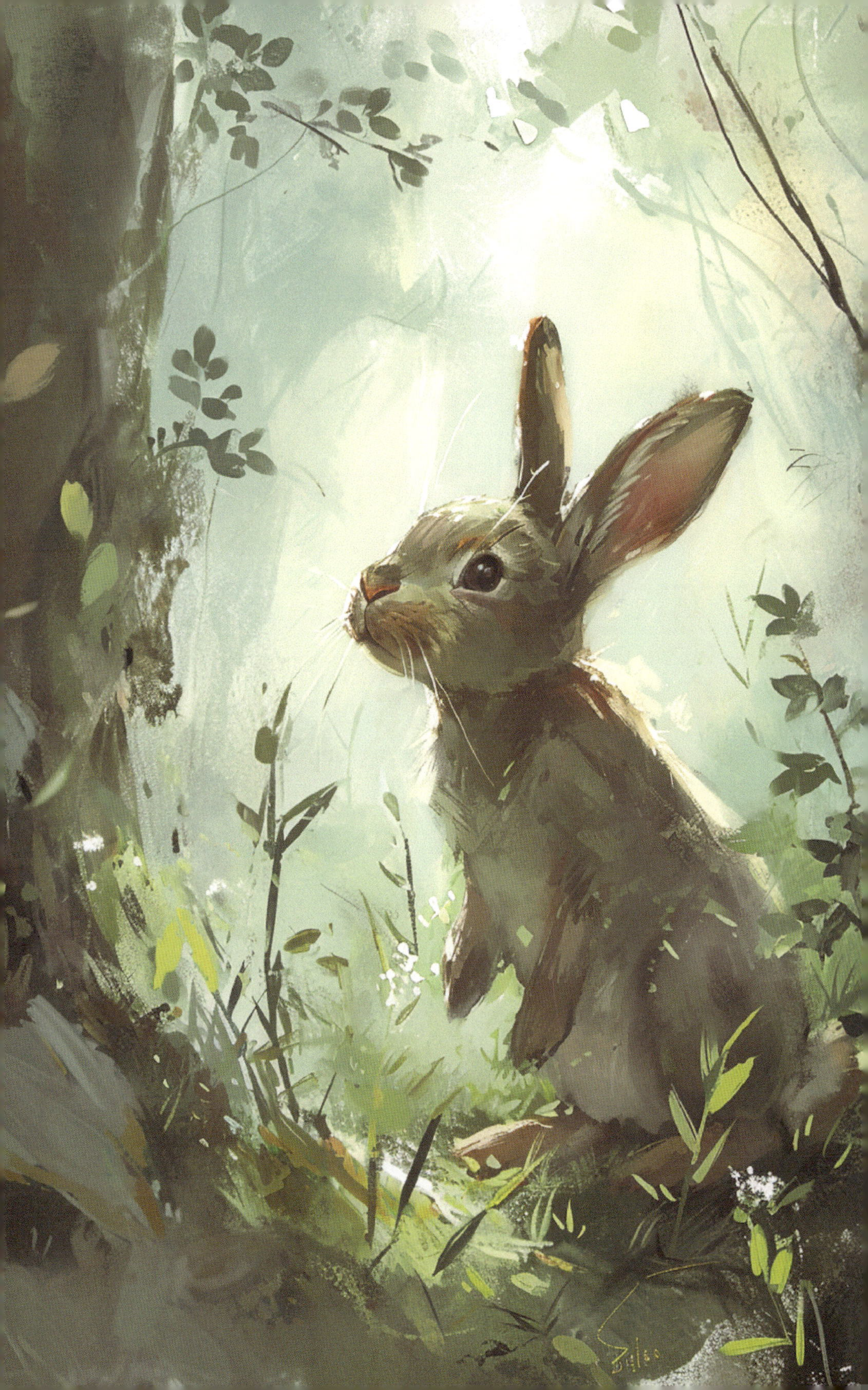

"So, Tao is like the energy that wakes up the forest?"
"所以,道就像是唤醒森林的能量？"

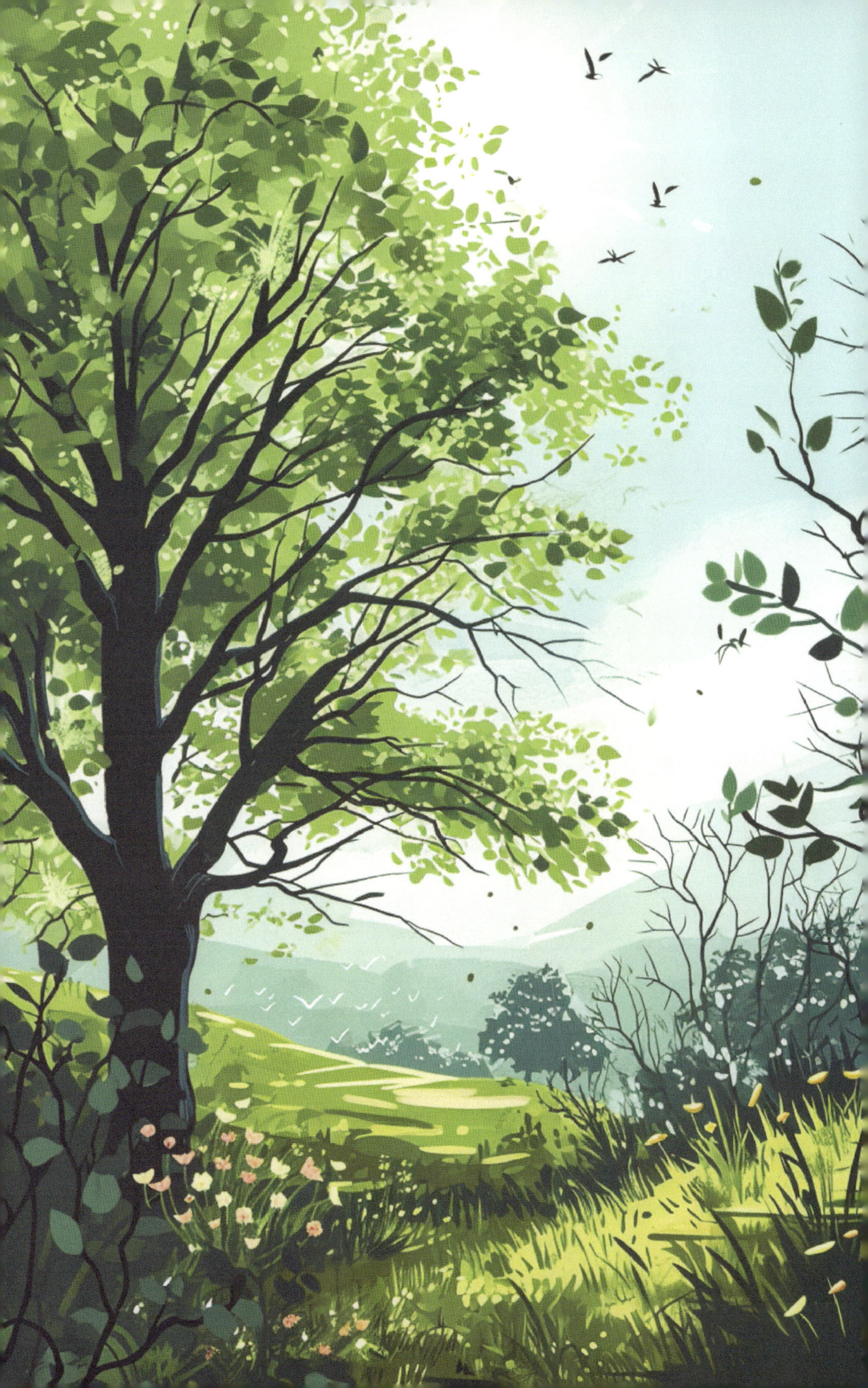

Master Ping nodded. "Yes, Bao. Tao is the life force in every sprout, every leaf. 平师傅点了点头。"是的，宝。道是每一株新芽、每一片叶子的生命力。

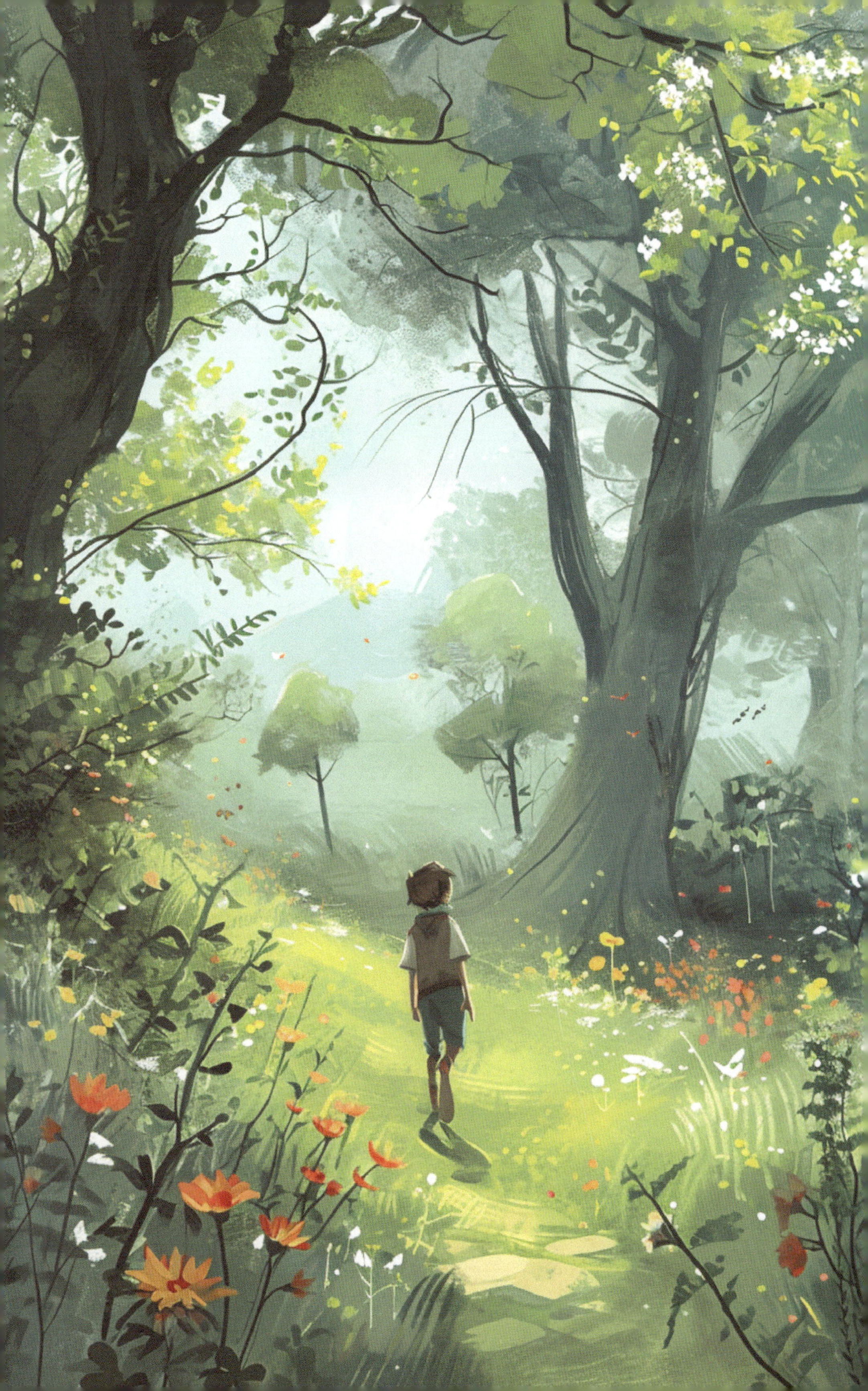

It is the unseen energy that guides the natural world."

它是引导自然世界的看不见的能量。"

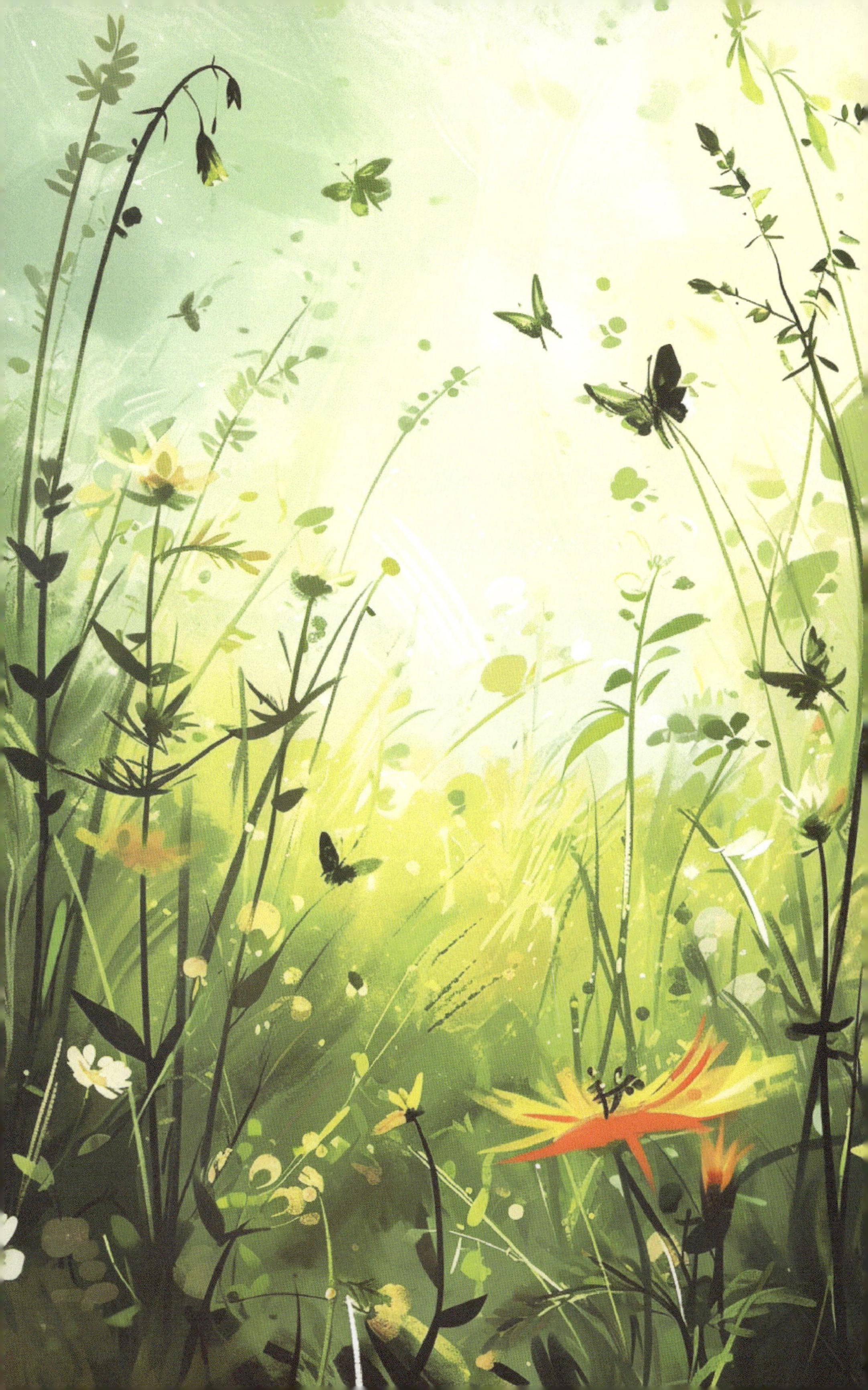

Chapter 2

-

The Summer of Growth

第二章

-

夏长

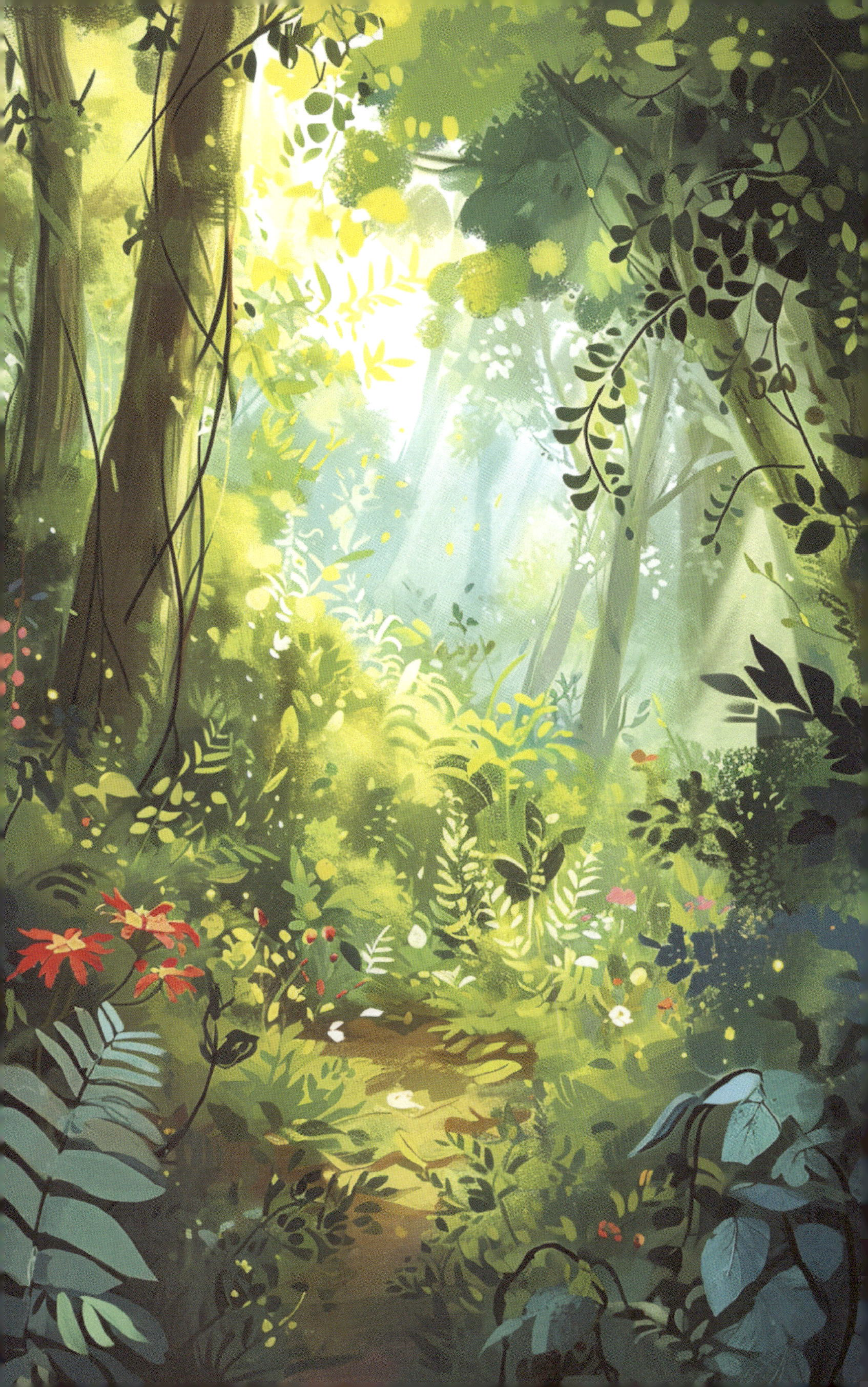

As the days grew warmer and the forest lush with greenery, 随着天气越来越暖和，森林里绿树成荫，

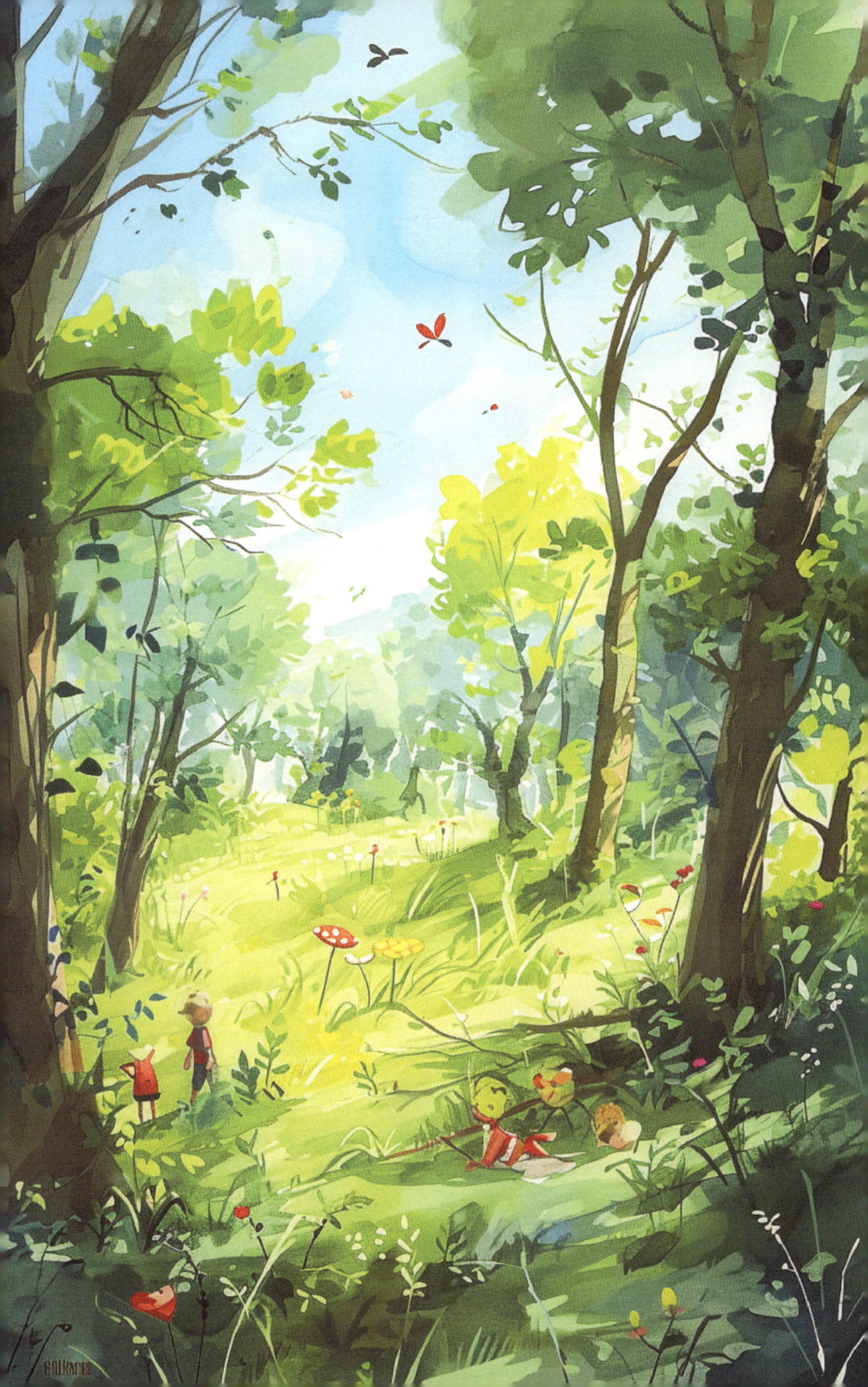

Master Ping spoke of Tao in summer.
平师傅在夏天说起了道。

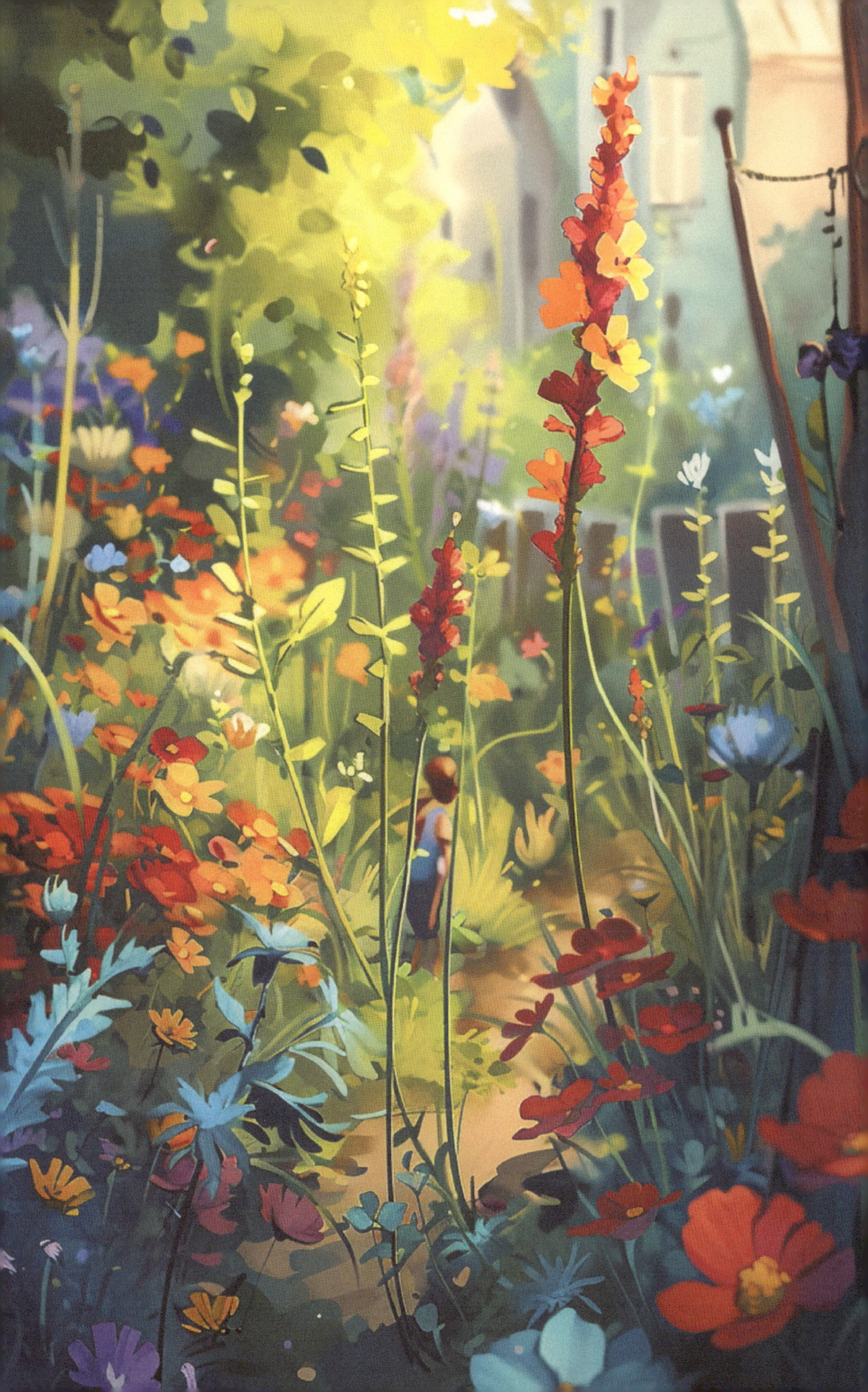

"Now, the forest is in its full glory," he said. "现在，这片森林正处于它的辉煌之中，"他说。

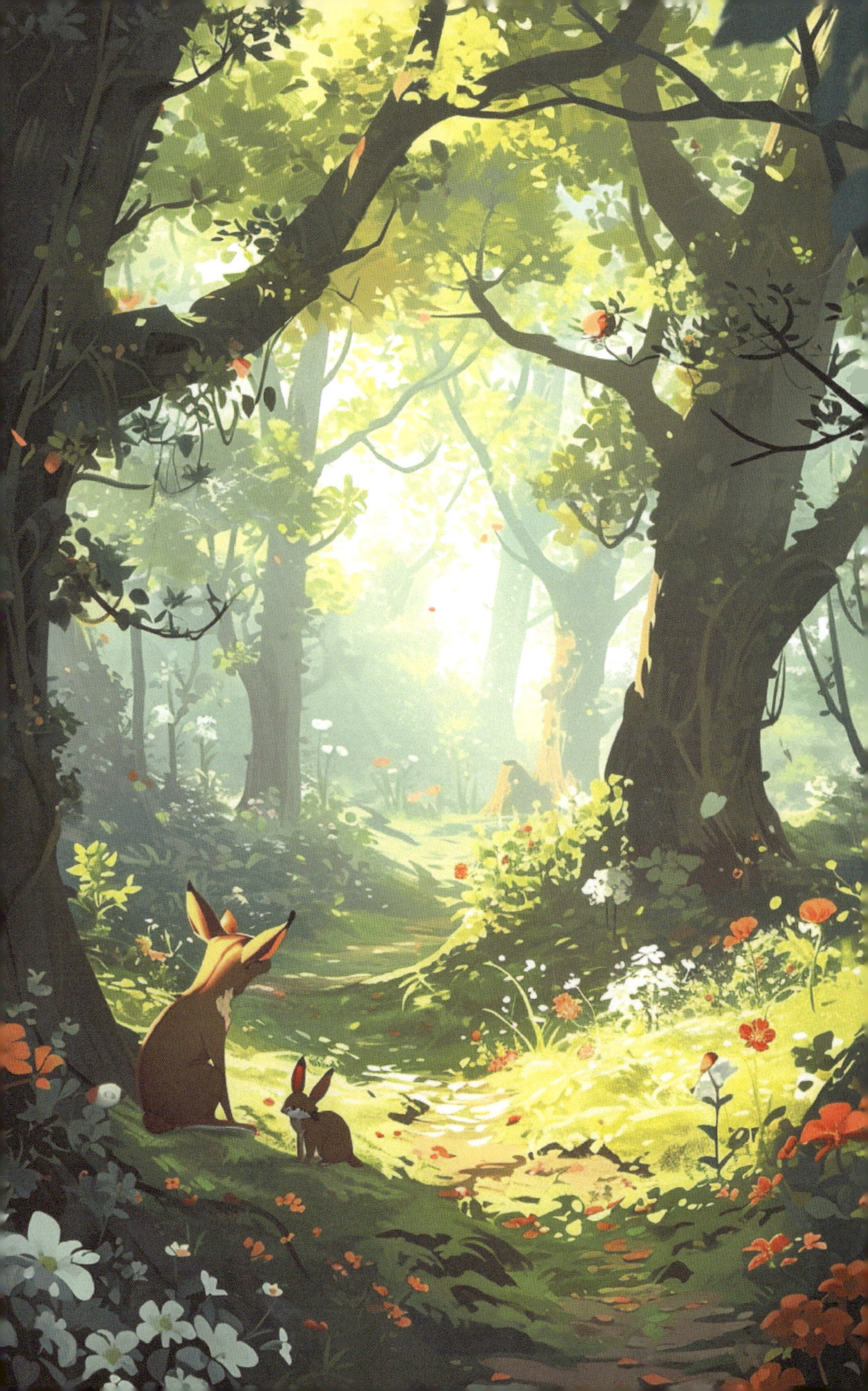

"The trees are tall, the flowers bloom,
树木高大，鲜花盛开，

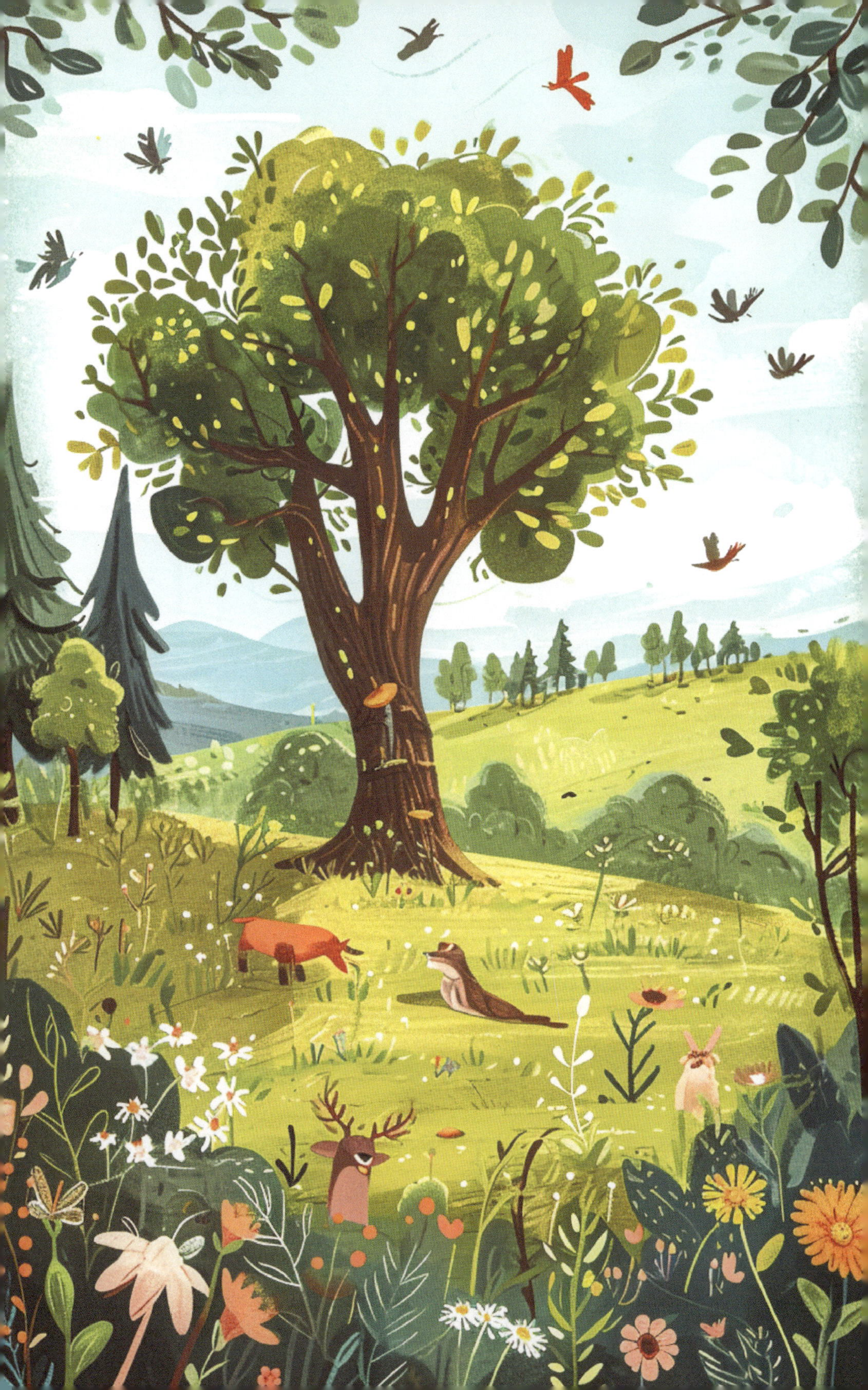

and the animals play under the sun.
动物们在阳光下玩耍。

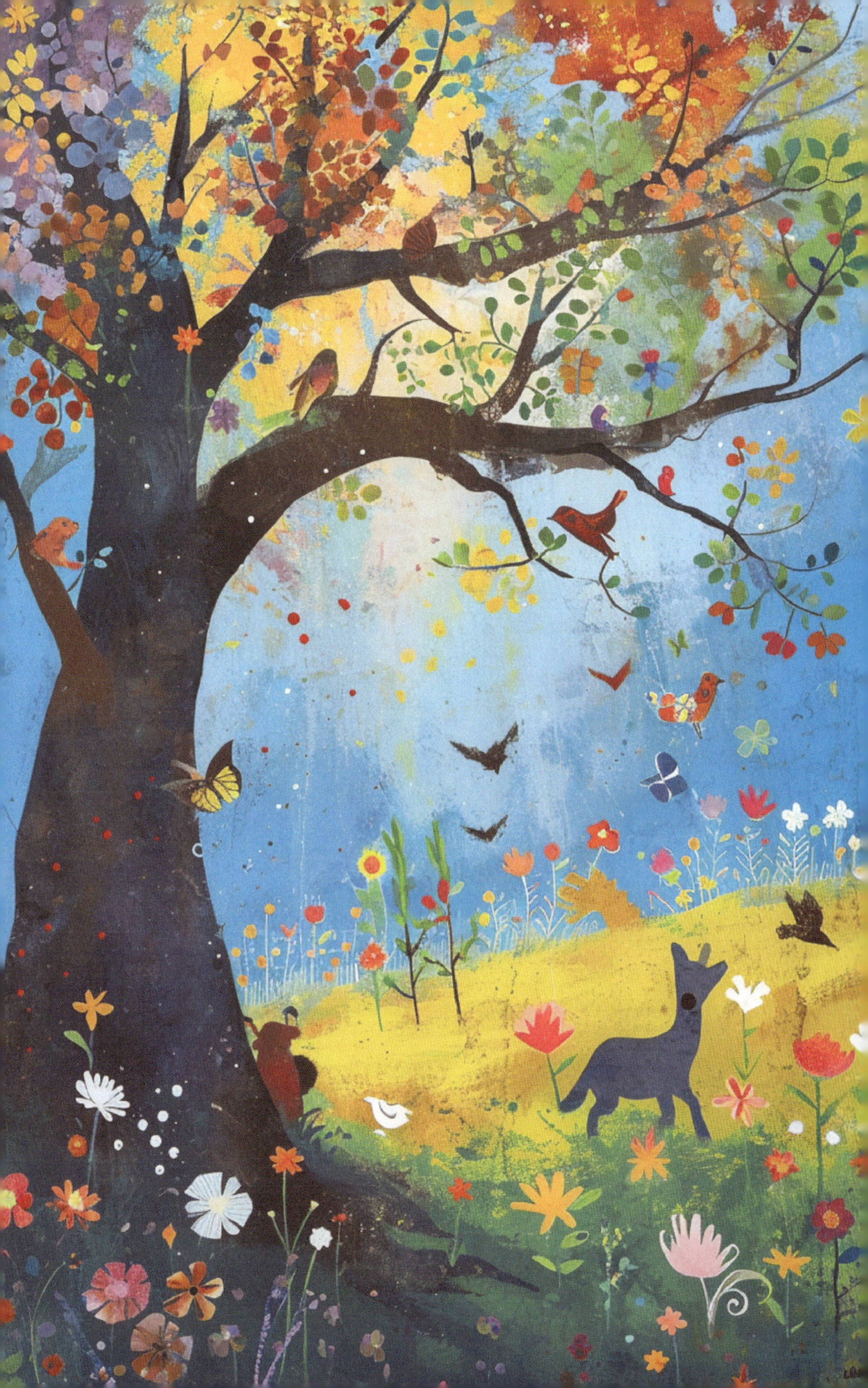

Summer is the time of growth and vitality,
夏天是成长和活力的季节

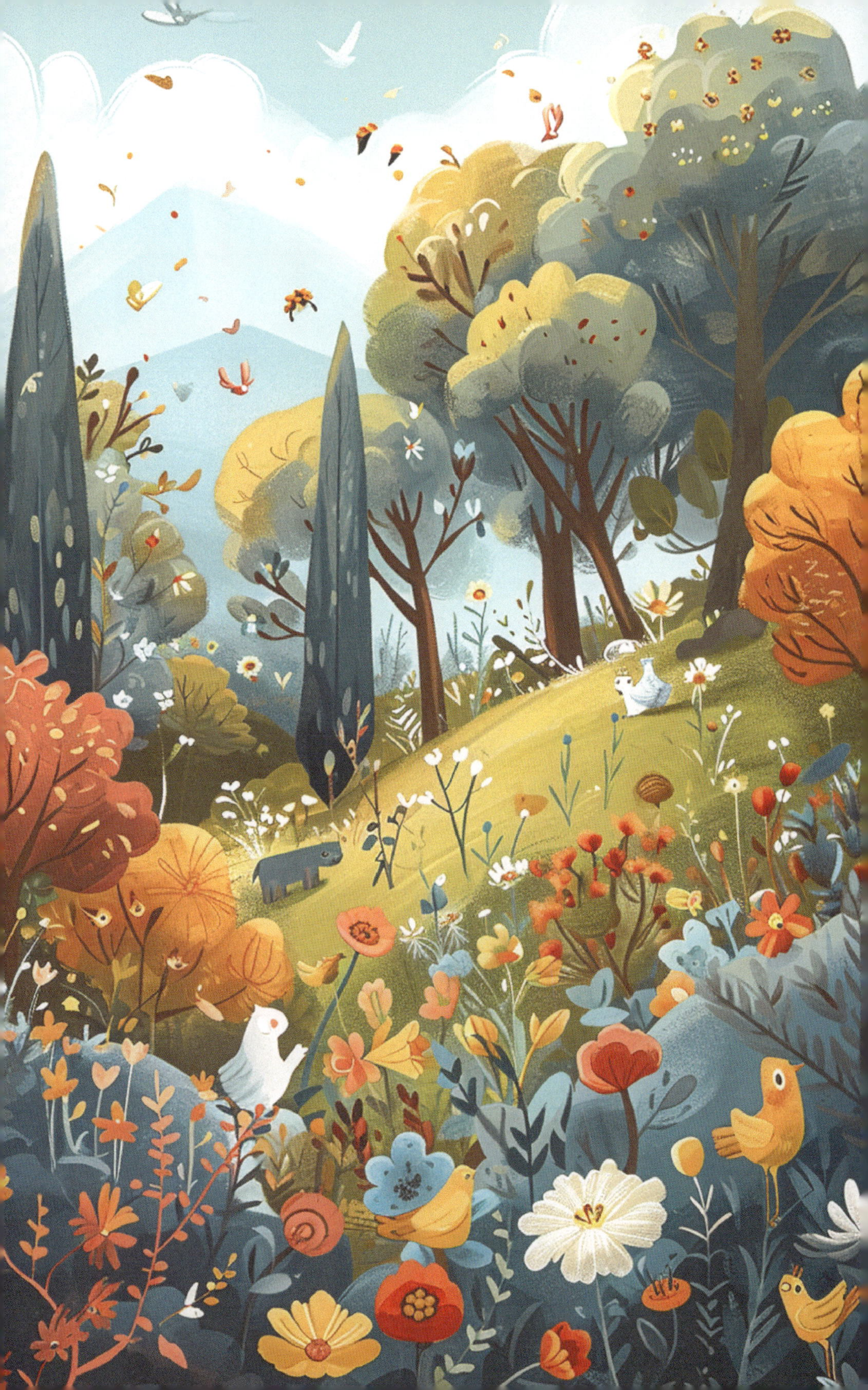

a time when Tao's energy is most apparent."
这是道的能量最明显的时期。"

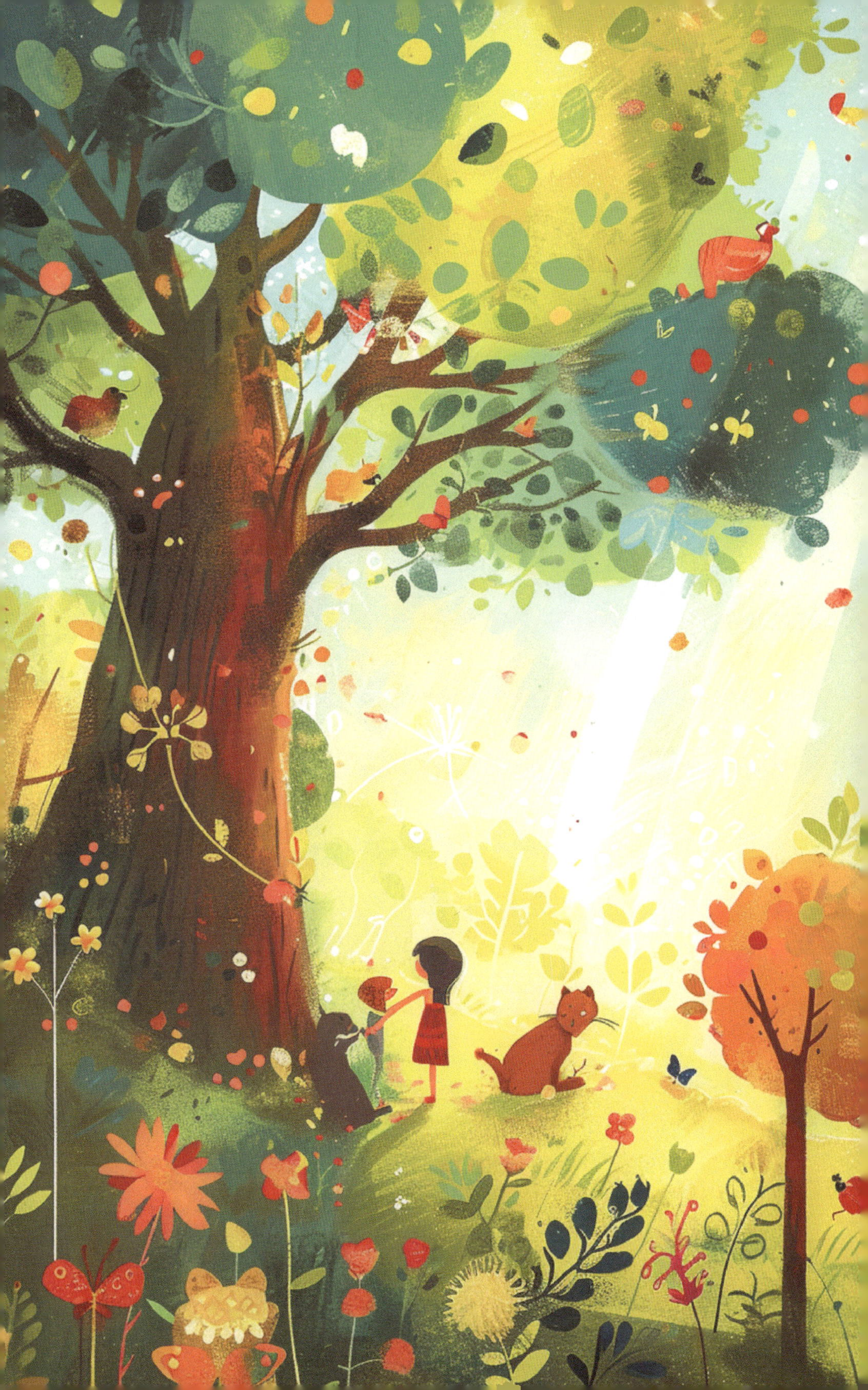

Luna, a young deer, gazed at the blooming flowers.

露娜，一只小鹿，凝视着盛开的花朵。

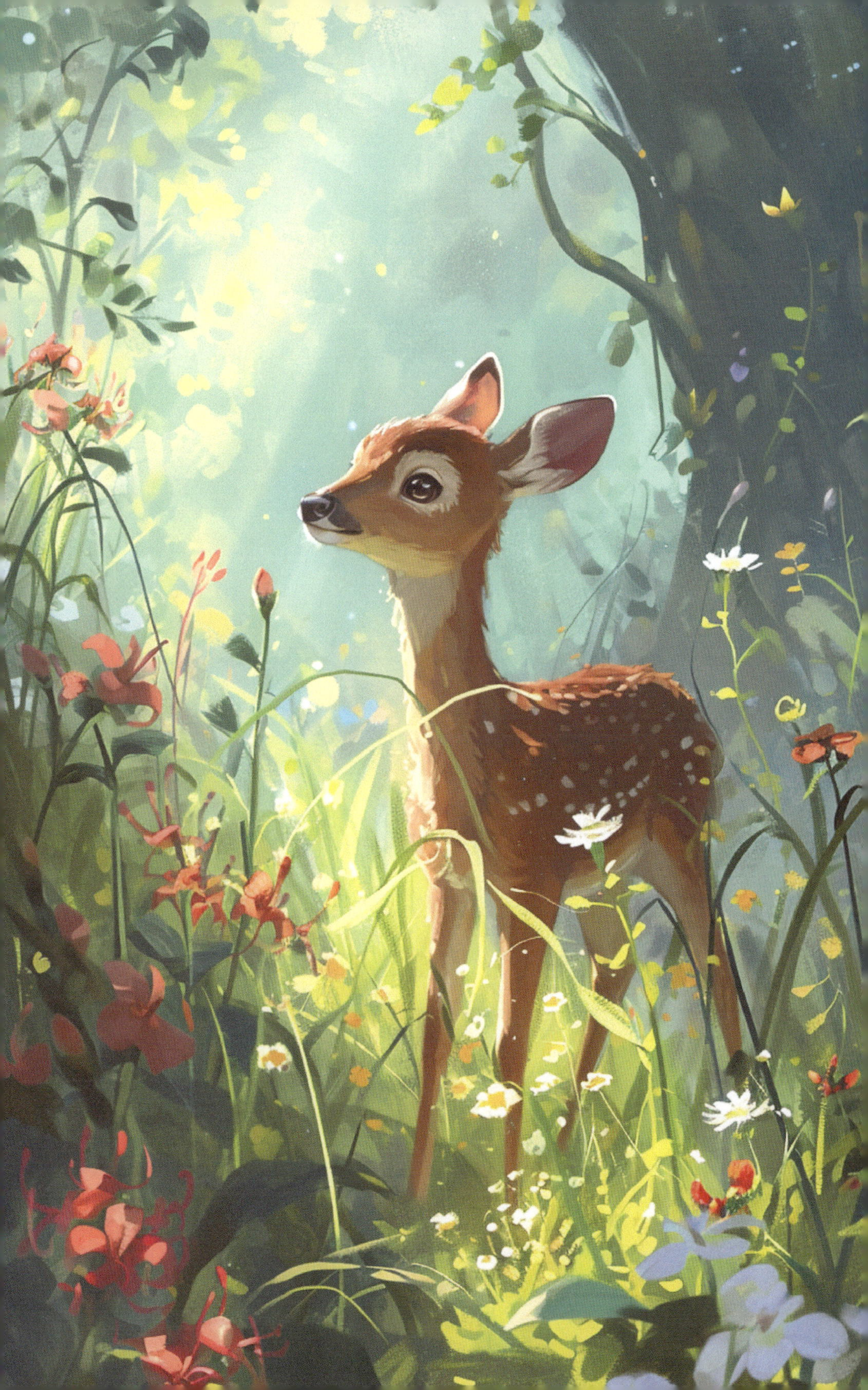

"Is Tao the reason these flowers are so colorful and lively?"
"道是这些花如此丰富多彩和活泼生动的原因吗？"

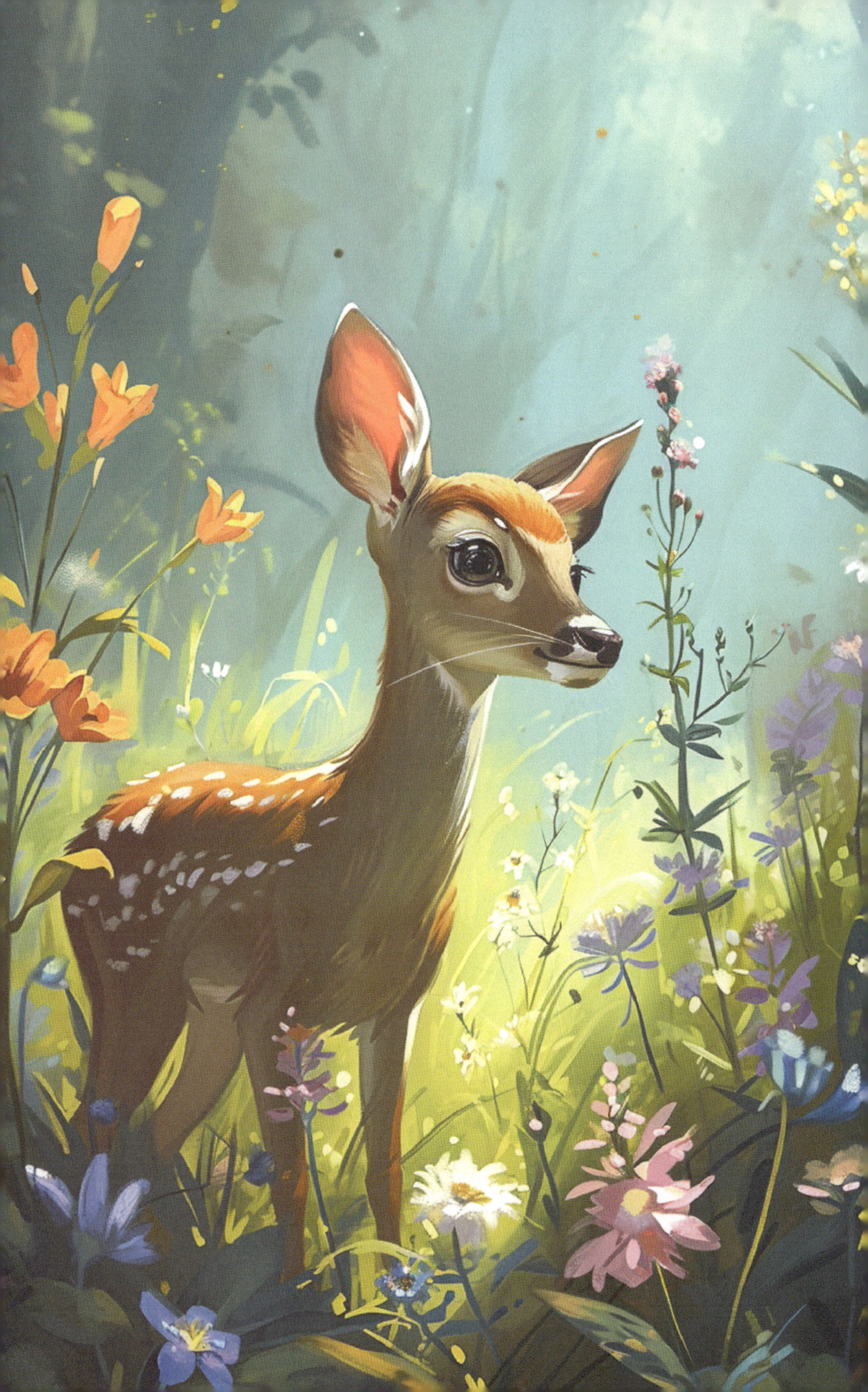

"Yes, Luna," Master Ping replied.

"是的，露娜，"平师傅回答道。

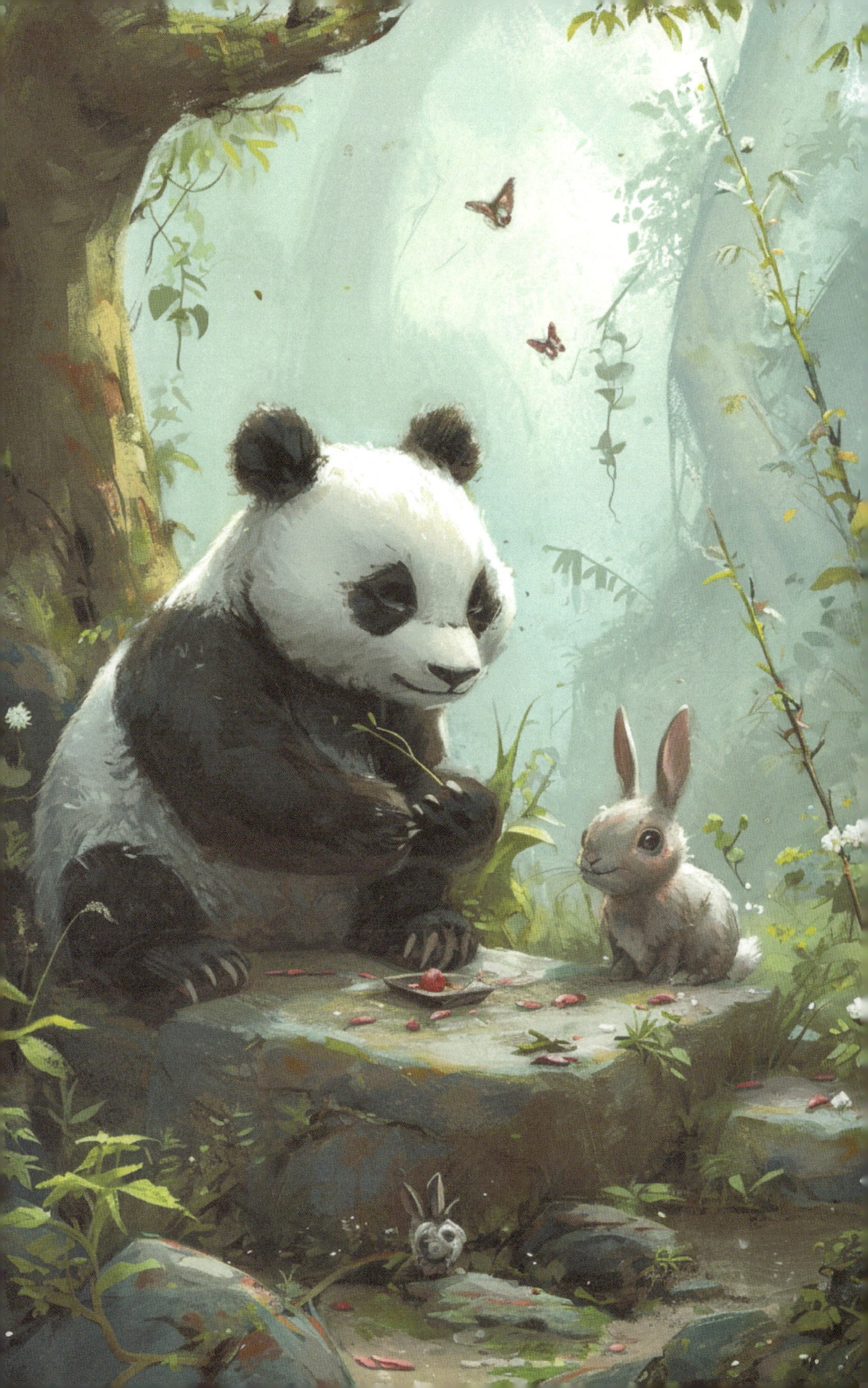

"Tao nurtures and sustains all life,
"道滋养和维持一切生命,

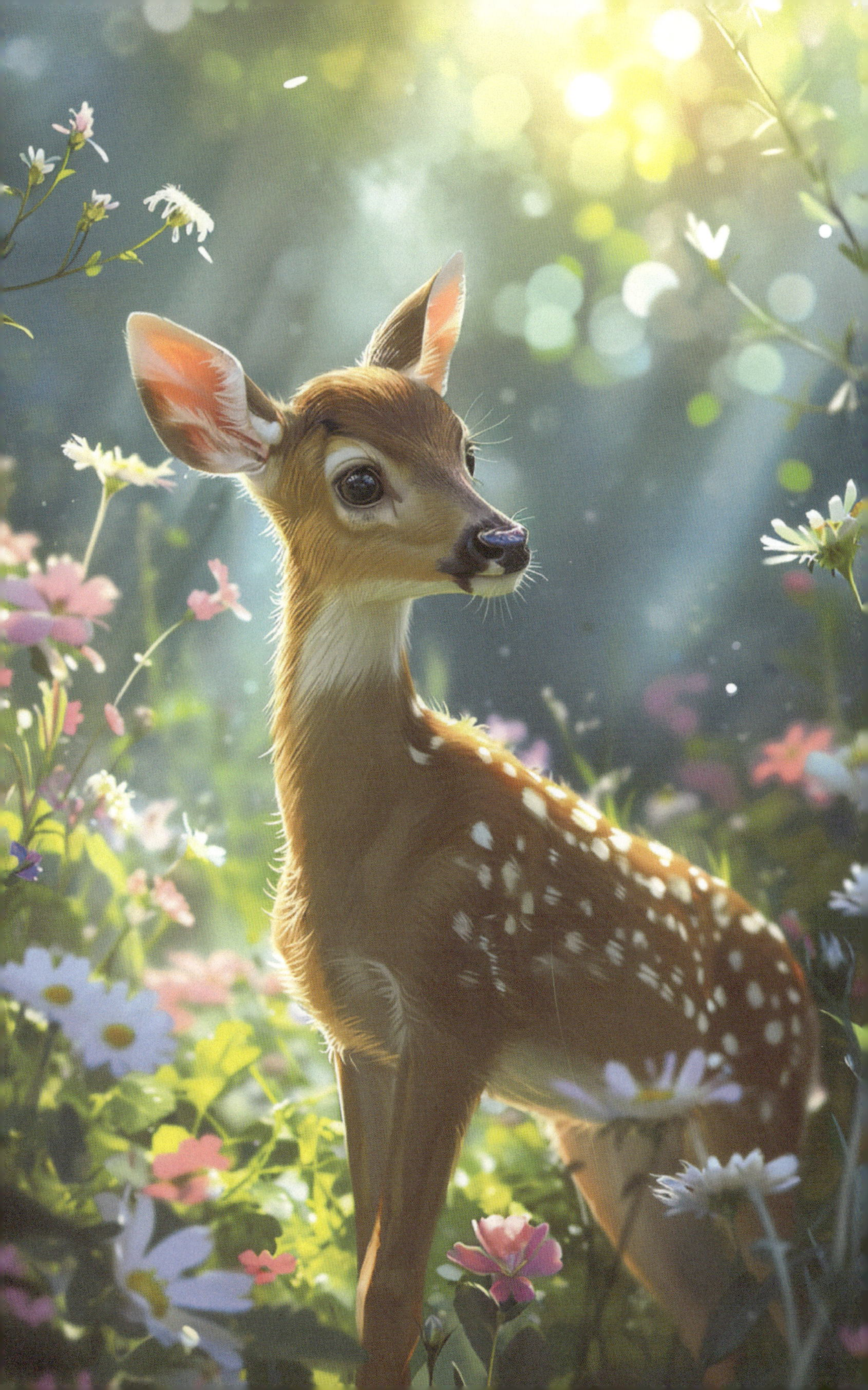

giving it the strength and energy to flourish."
赋予它蓬勃发展的力量和能量。"

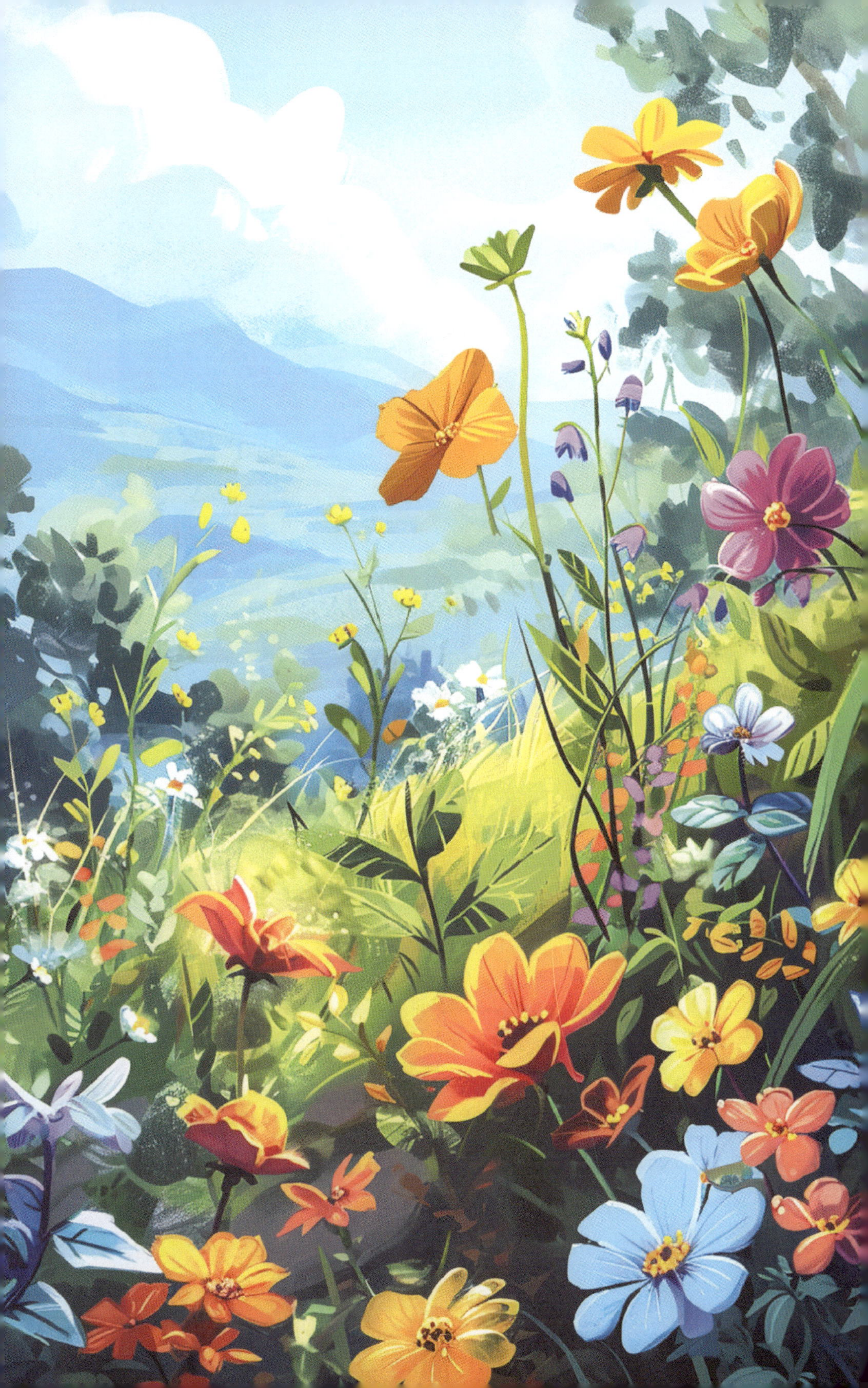

Chapter 3

-

The Autumn of Harvest

第三章

-

秋收

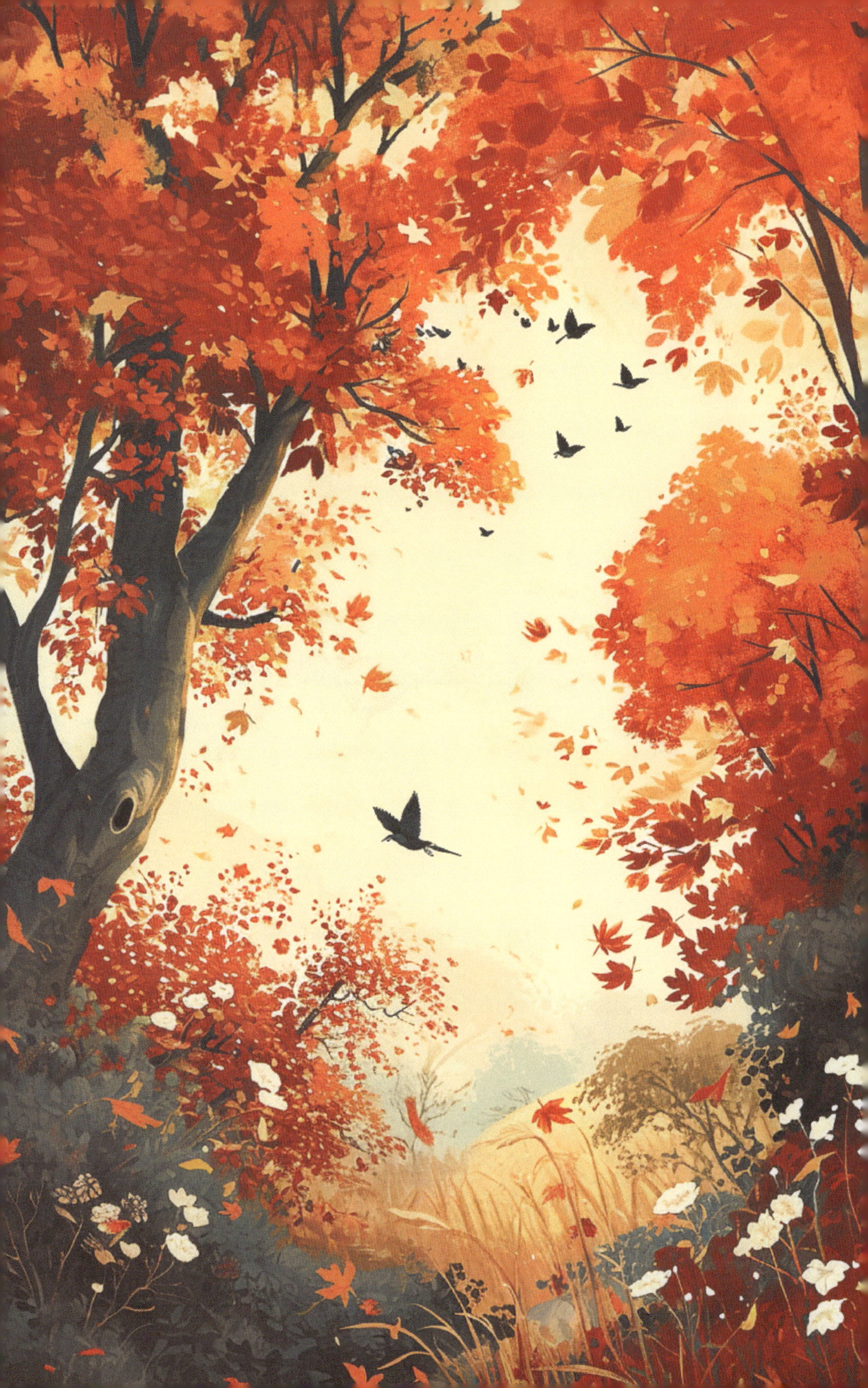

As the leaves turned golden and the air grew crisp,
随着树叶变成金黄色，空气变得清新，

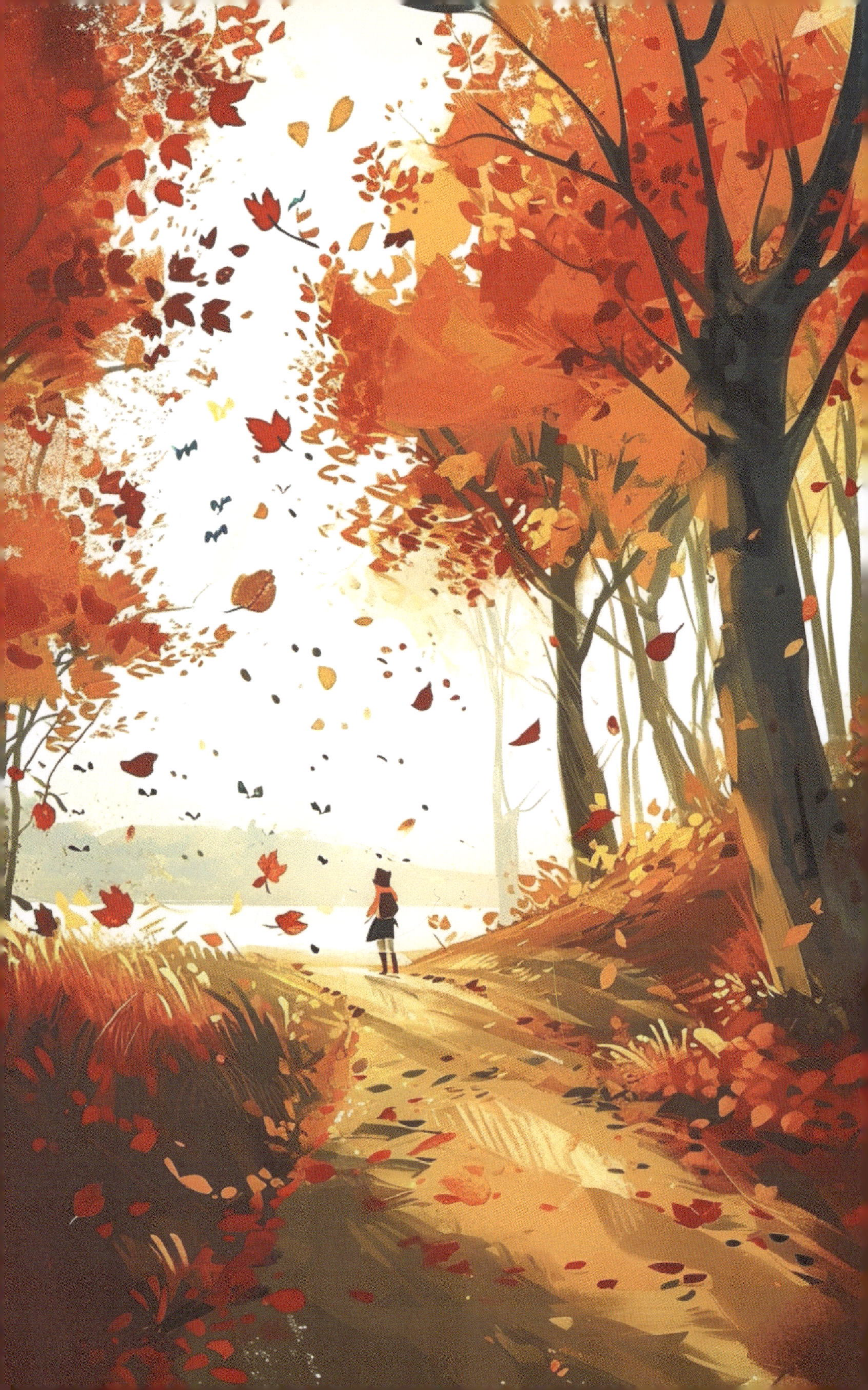

Master Ping taught about the Tao of autumn.
平师傅讲授秋天的道。

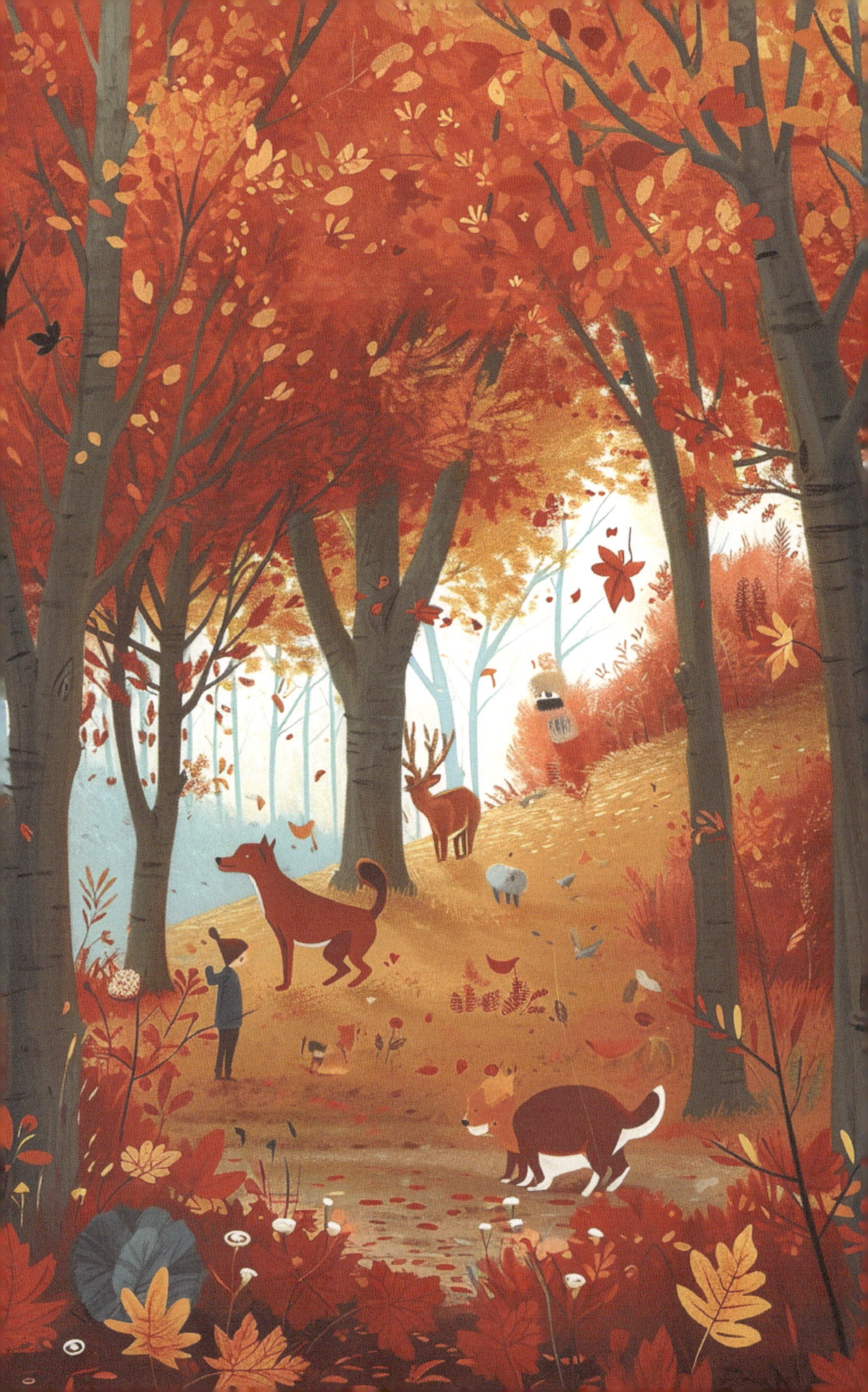

"This is the season of harvest," he said.
"这是收获的季节，"他说。

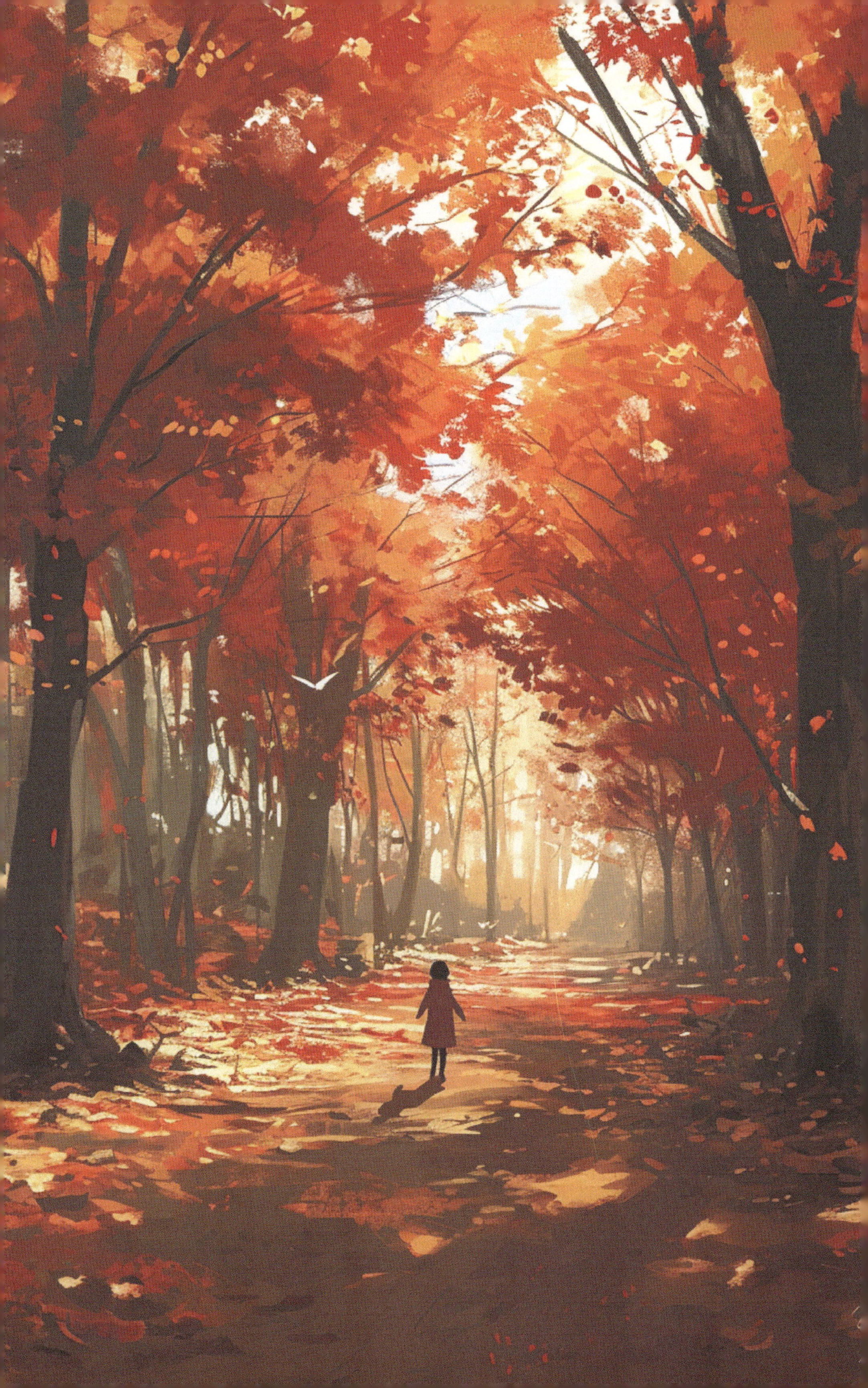

"The trees shed their leaves,
"树落下叶子,

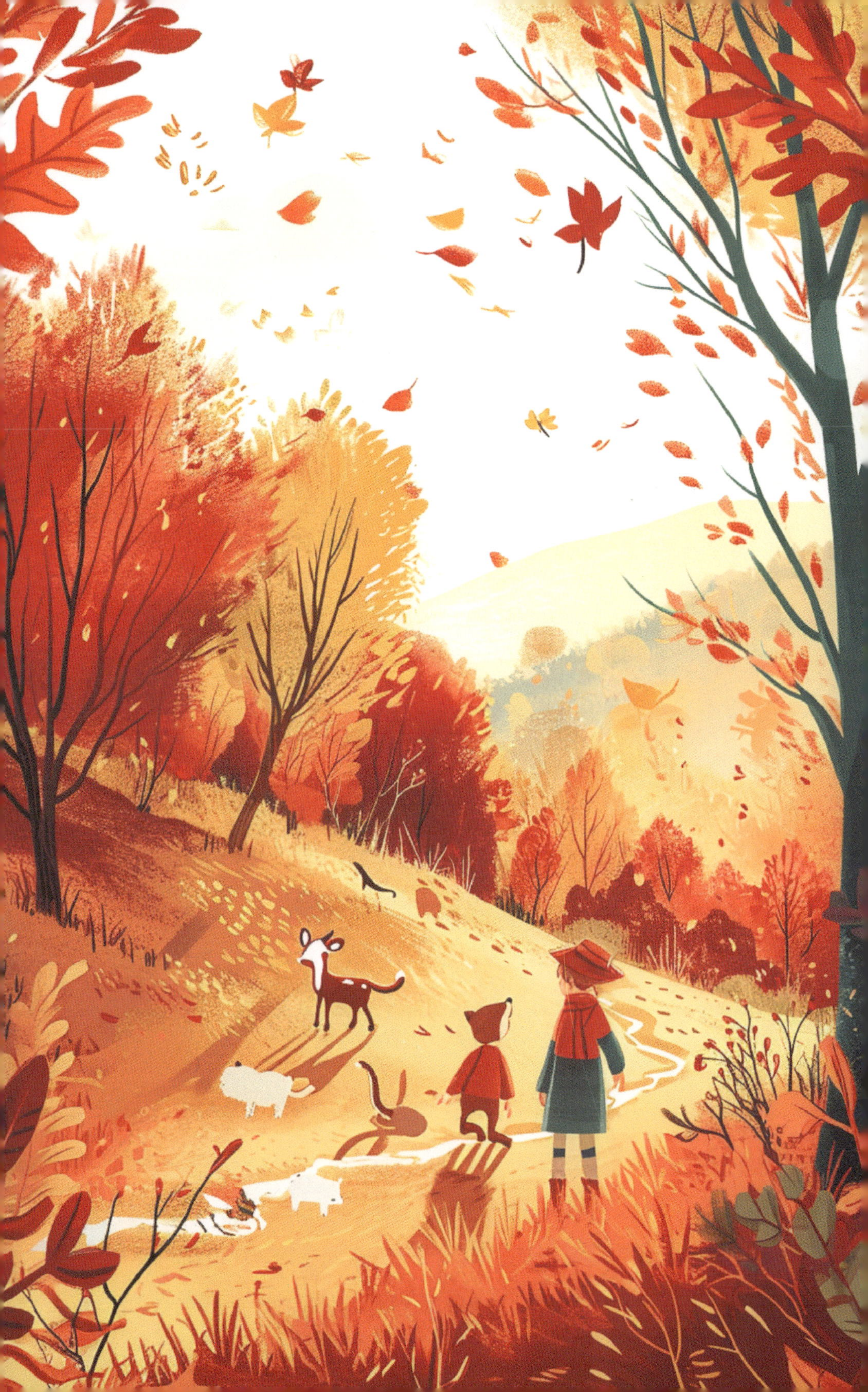

and the animals prepare for the winter.
动物们为冬天做准备。

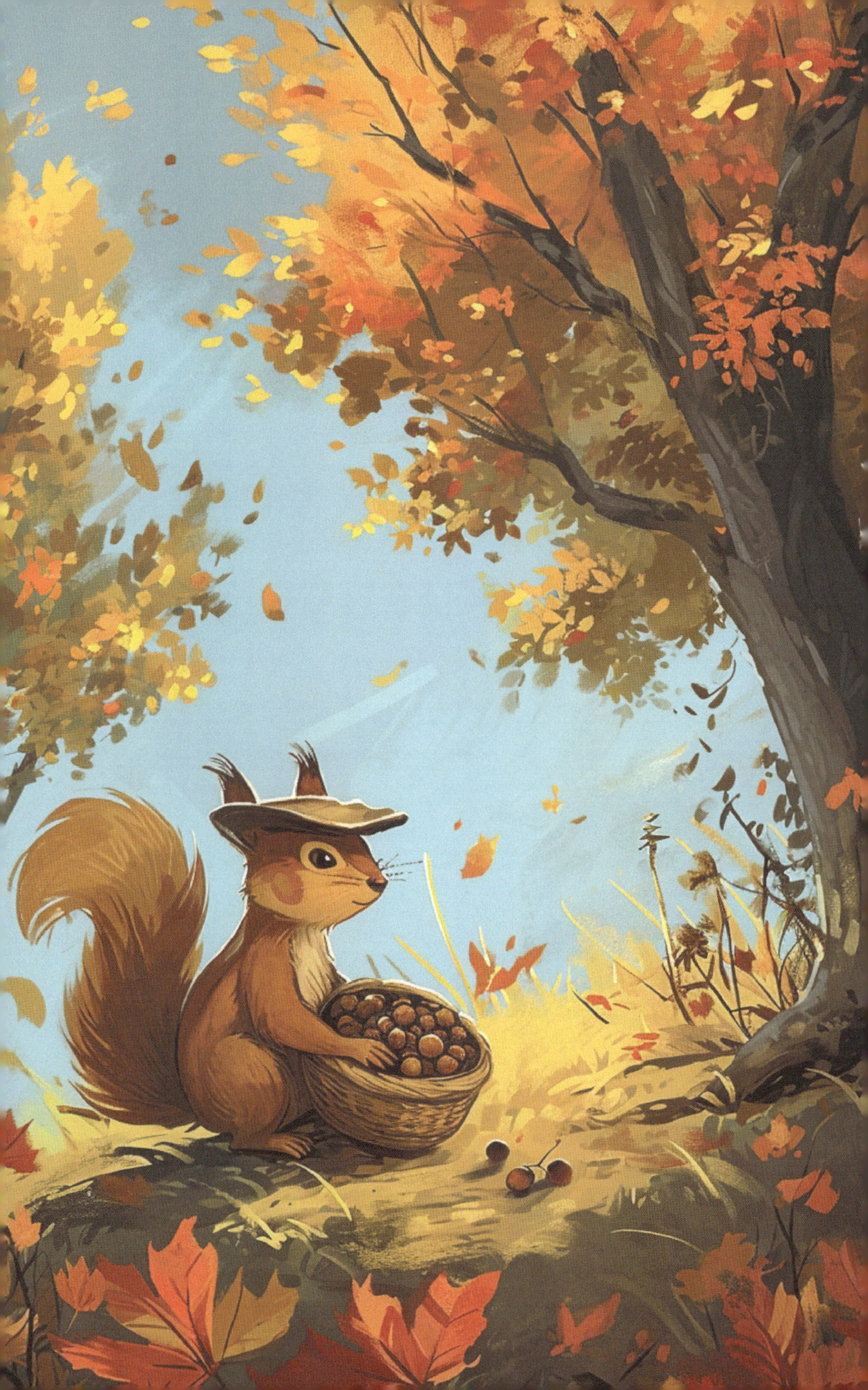

Autumn teaches us about balance and letting go.
秋天教会我们平衡和放手。

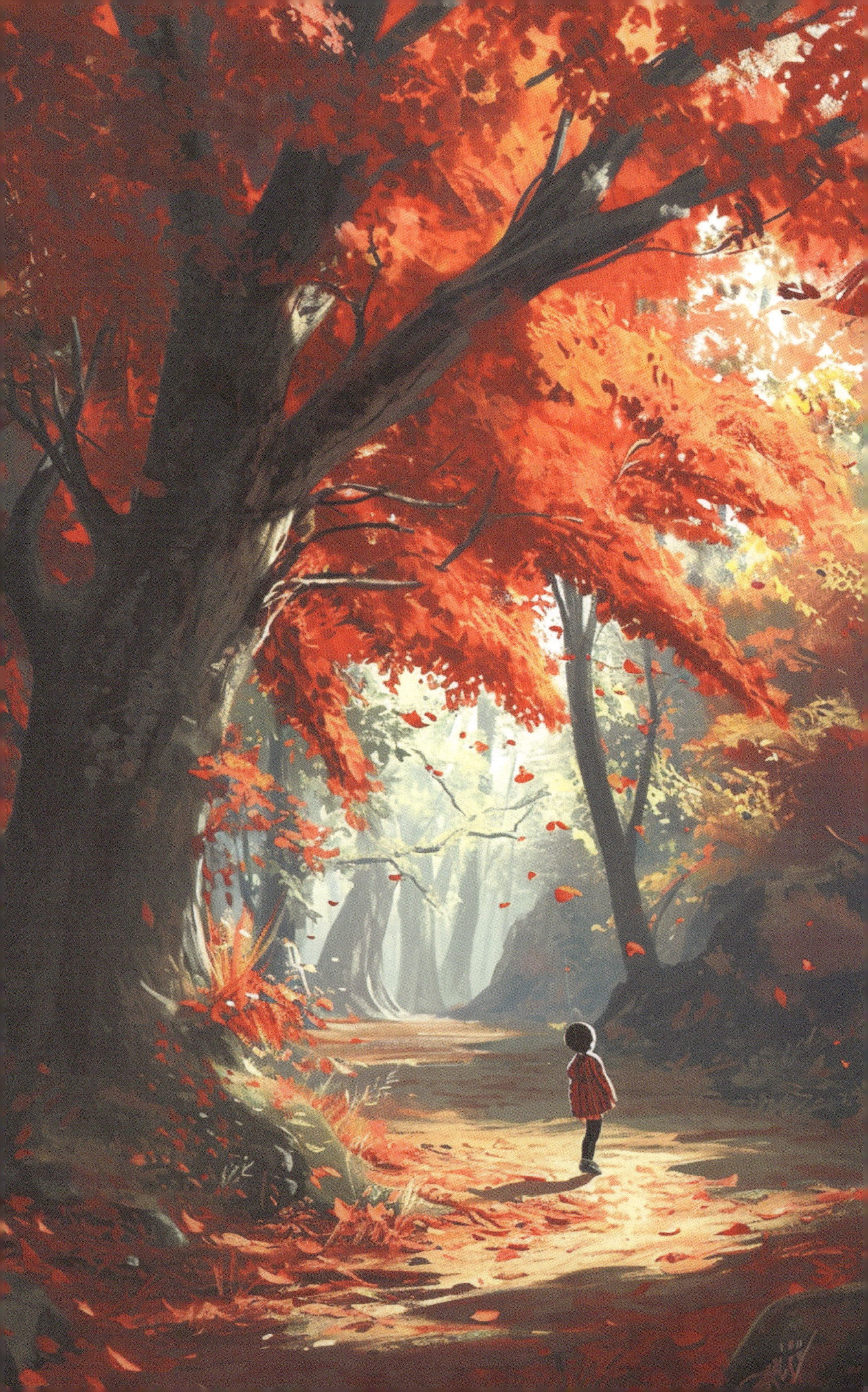

Tao reminds us that everything has its time."

道提醒我们，万事万物皆有其时。"

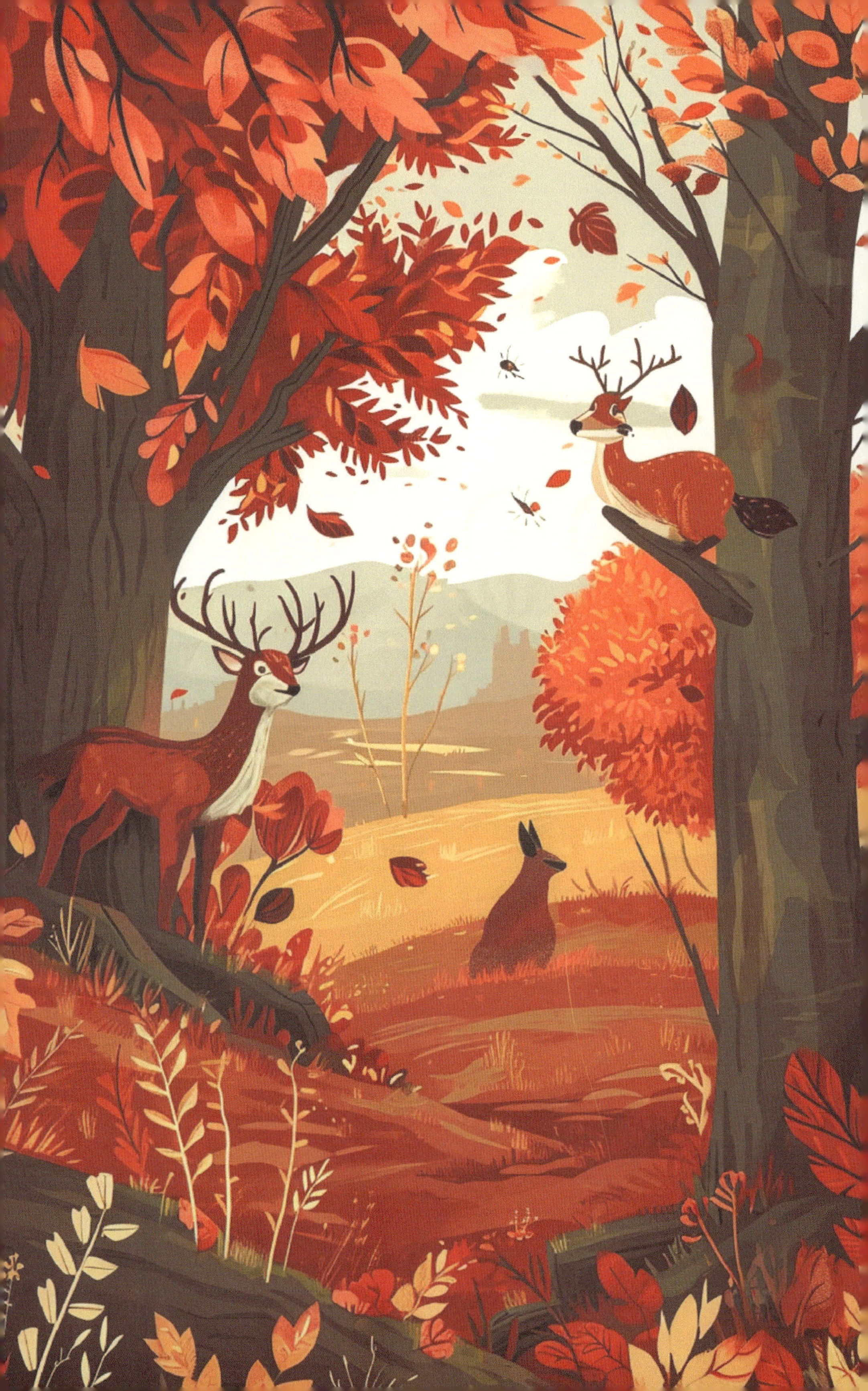

Tiko, a squirrel busy gathering acorns, paused to listen.
提科，一只忙着收集橡子的松鼠，停下来听。

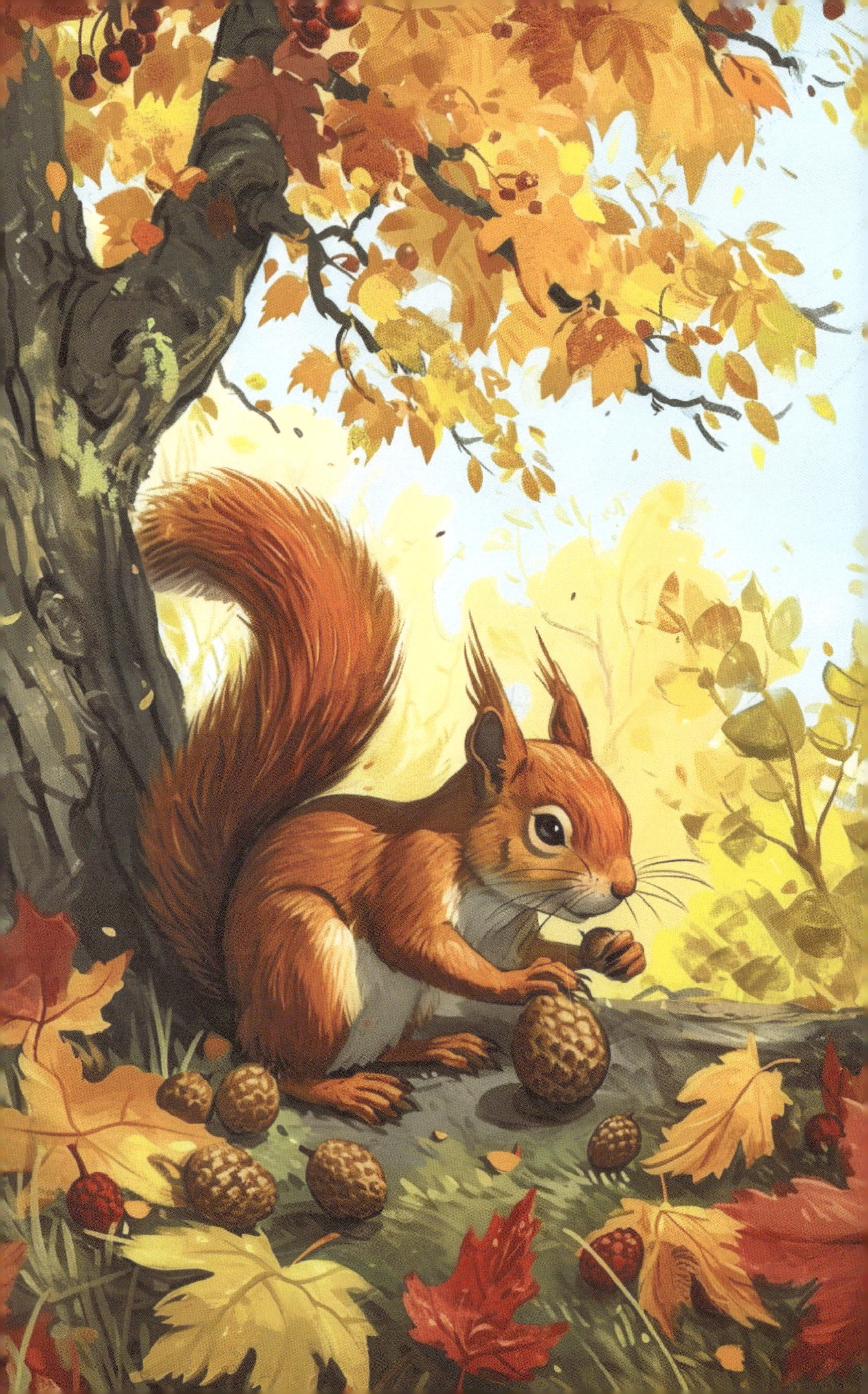

"So Tao is in the changing leaves and the cooling air?"
"所以道在叶子的颜色变化和凉爽的空气中？"

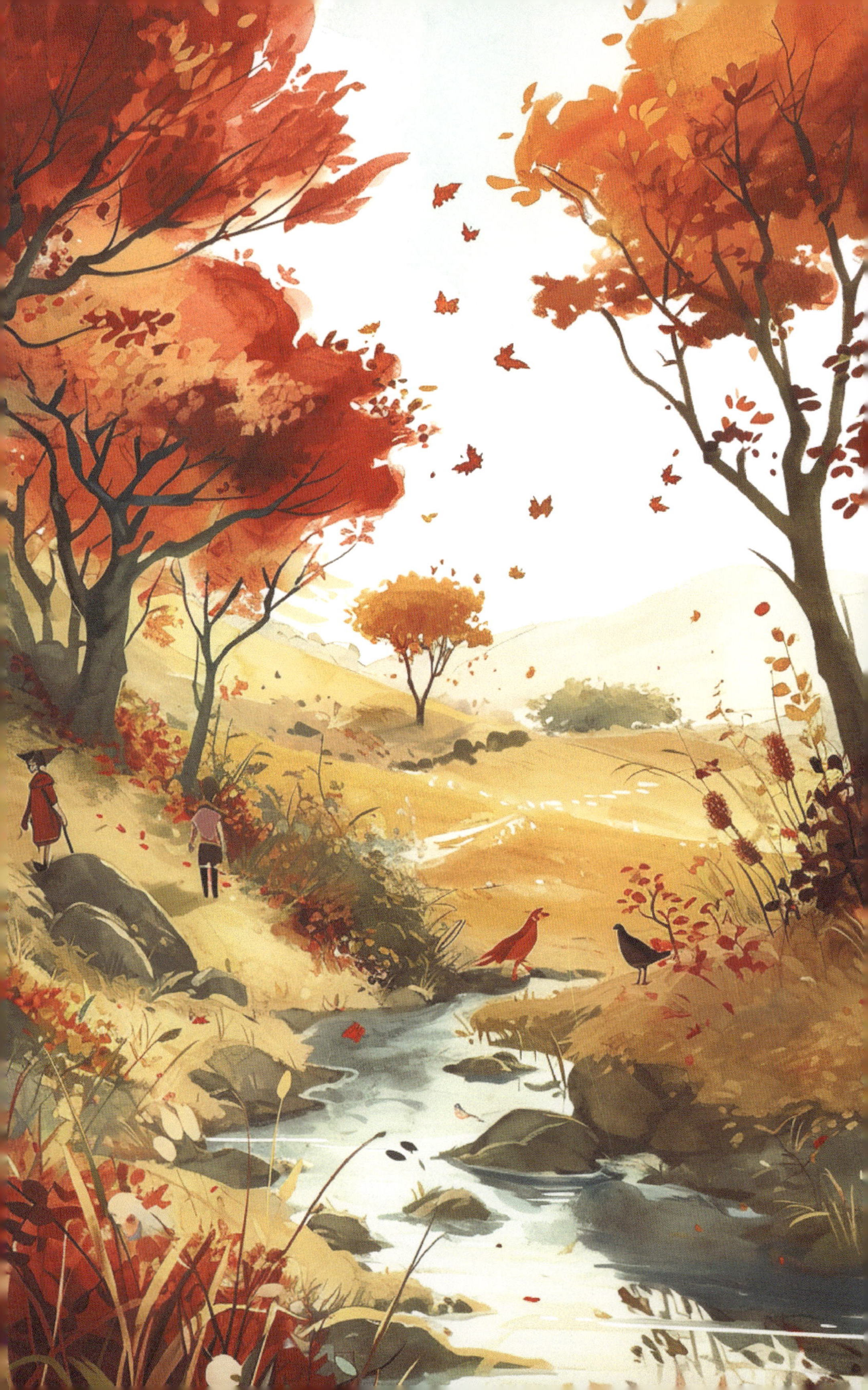

"Exactly, Tiko," Master Ping smiled.

"没错，提科，"平师傅笑了笑。

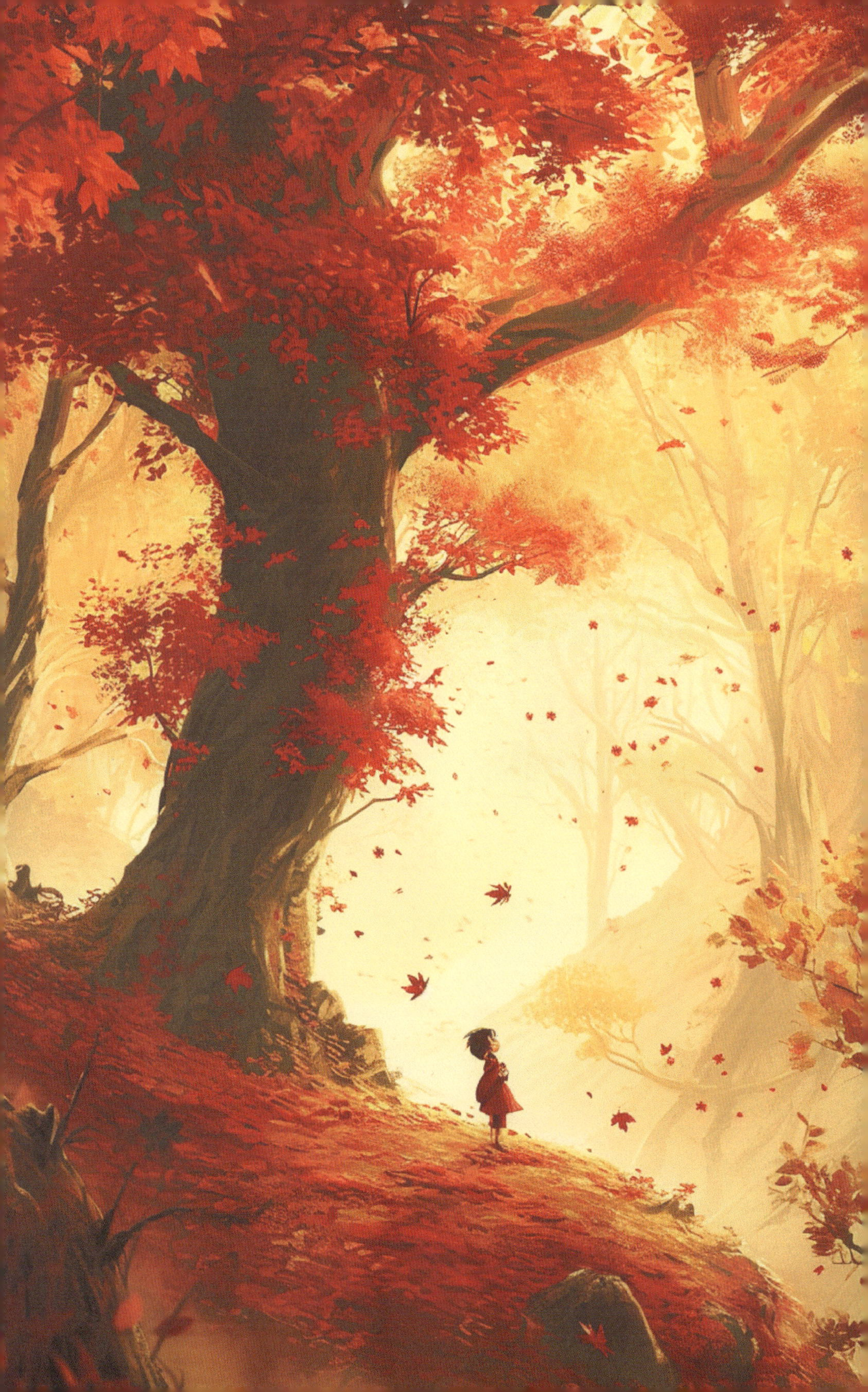

"Tao is in the cycle of life, in the change and flow of the seasons."
"道在生命的轮回中，在季节的变化和流动中。"

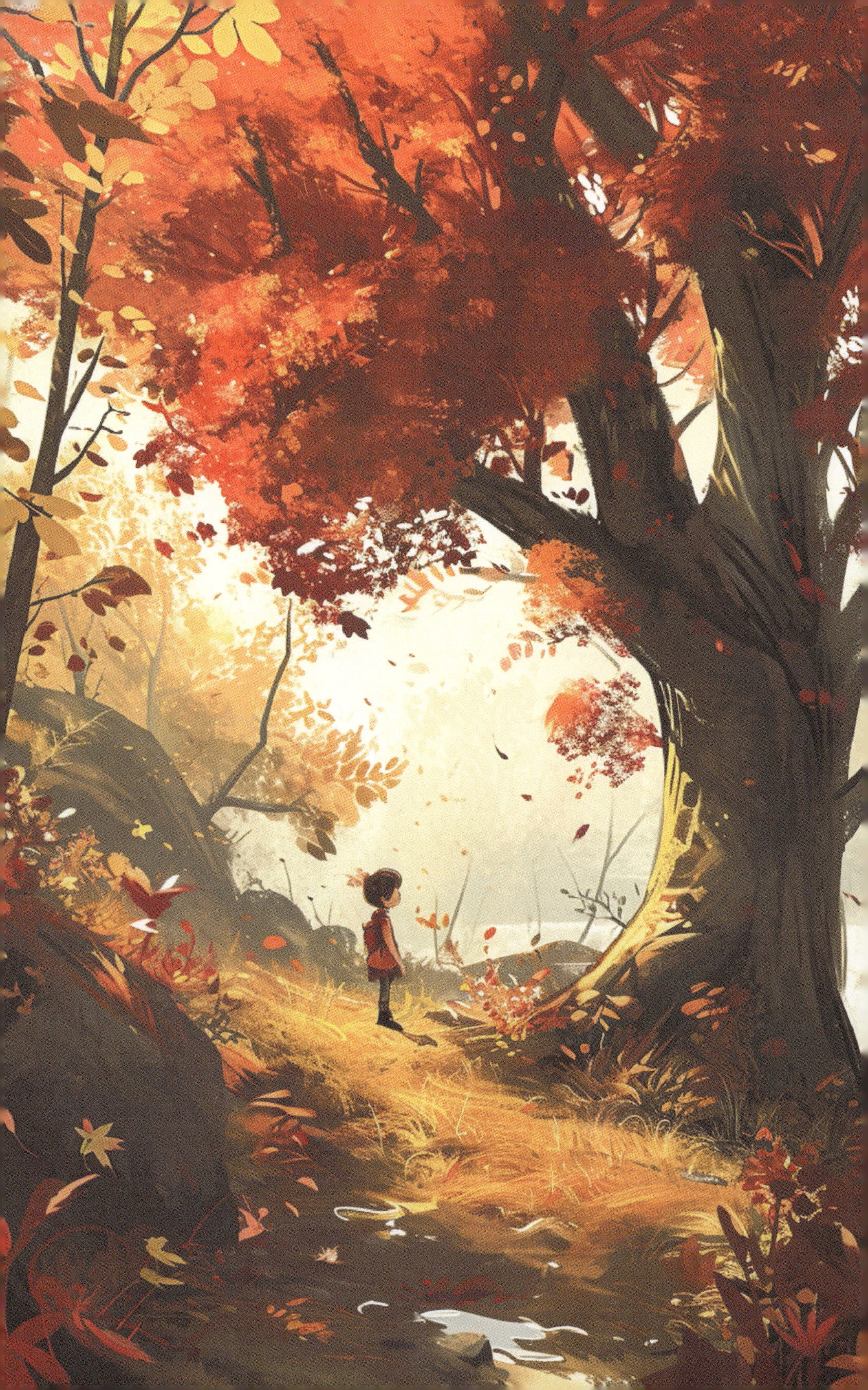

Chapter 4

-

The Winter of Stillness

第四章

-

冬藏

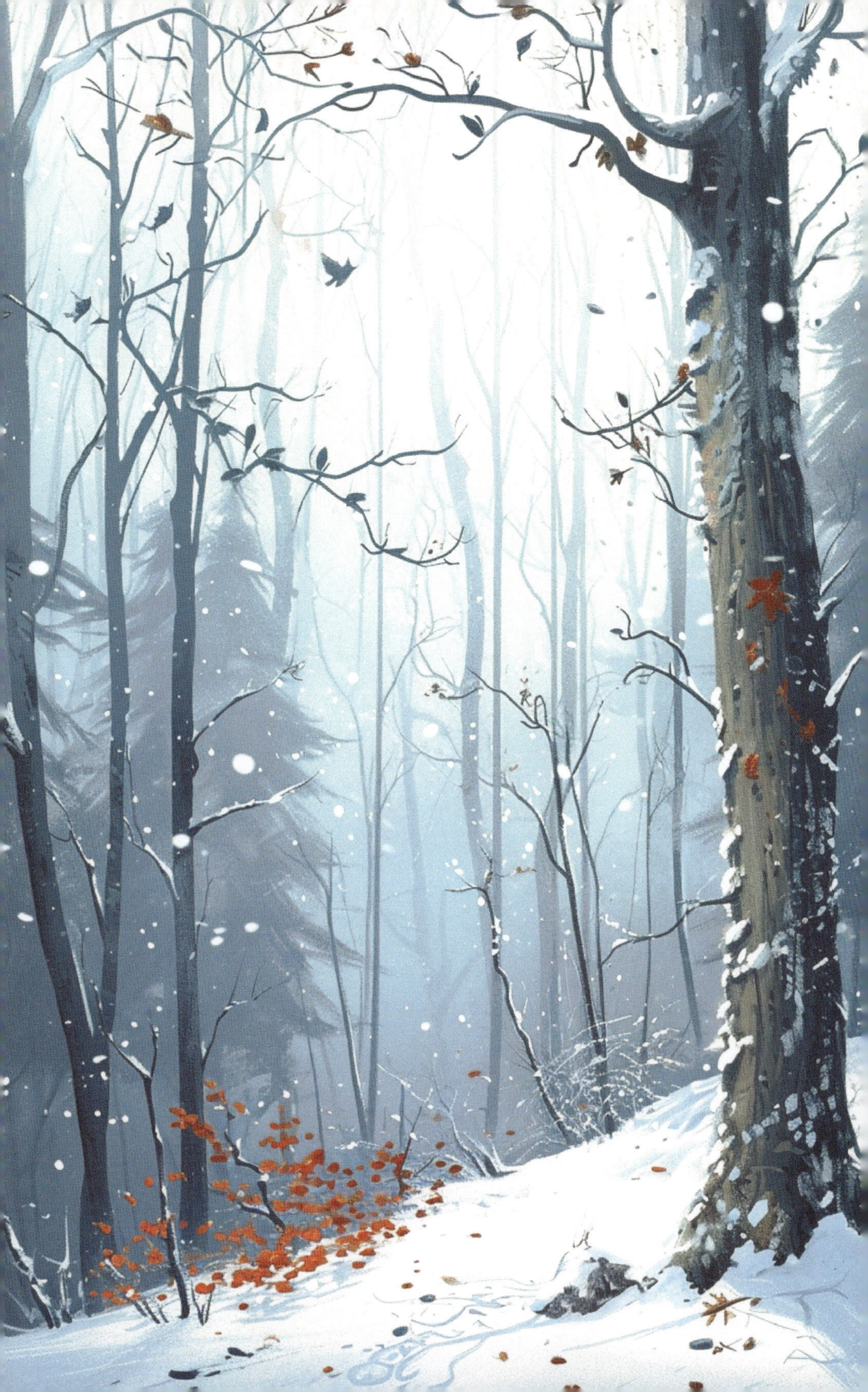

When winter cloaked the forest in white,
当冬天把森林披上白色的外衣时,

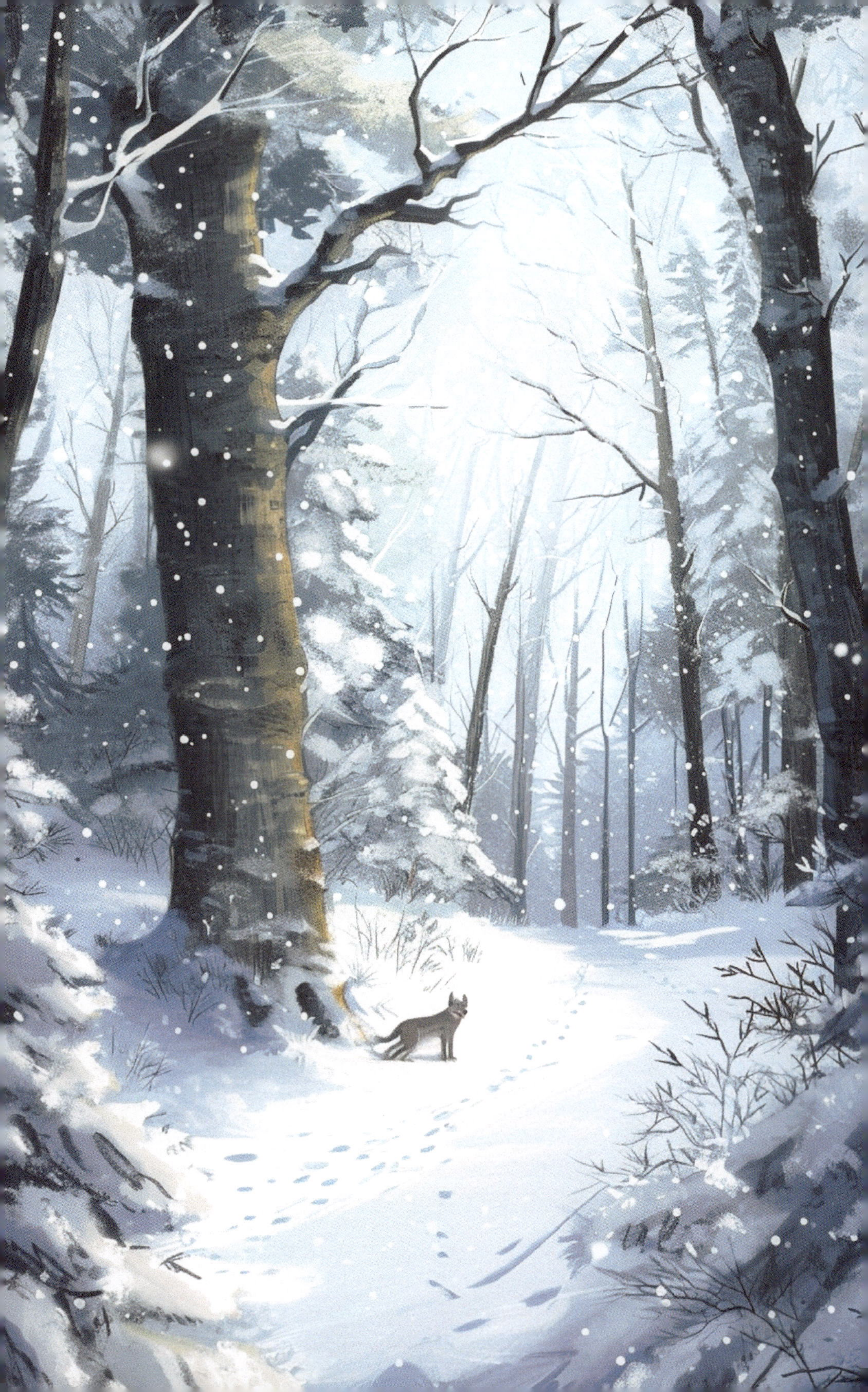

Master Ping spoke of Tao's quiet wisdom.
平师傅说起了道的安静的智慧。

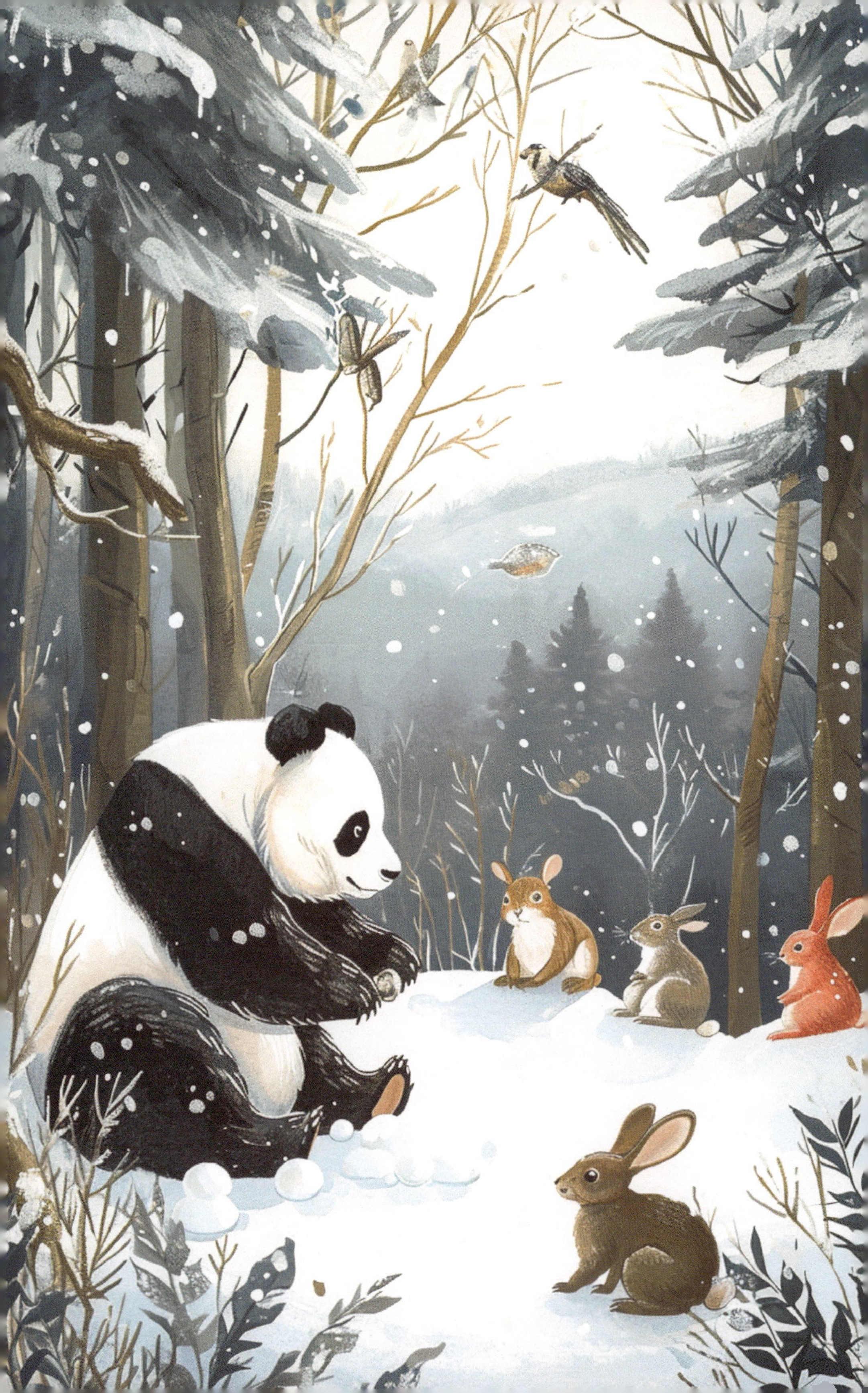

"Winter is a time of stillness and rest," he said.
"冬天是安静和休息的时期，"他说。

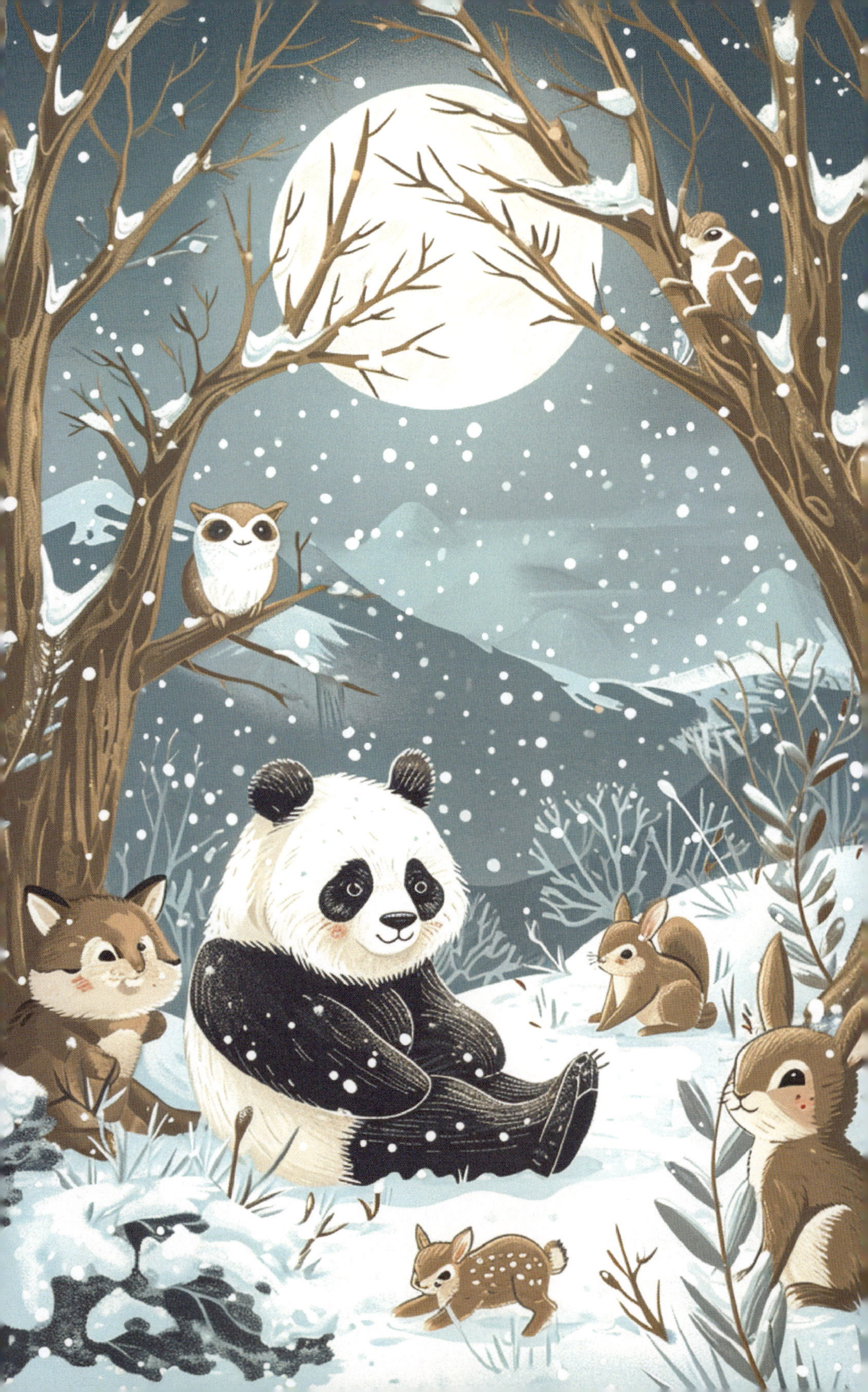

"The forest sleeps, and the animals rest.
"森林在睡觉,动物们在休息。

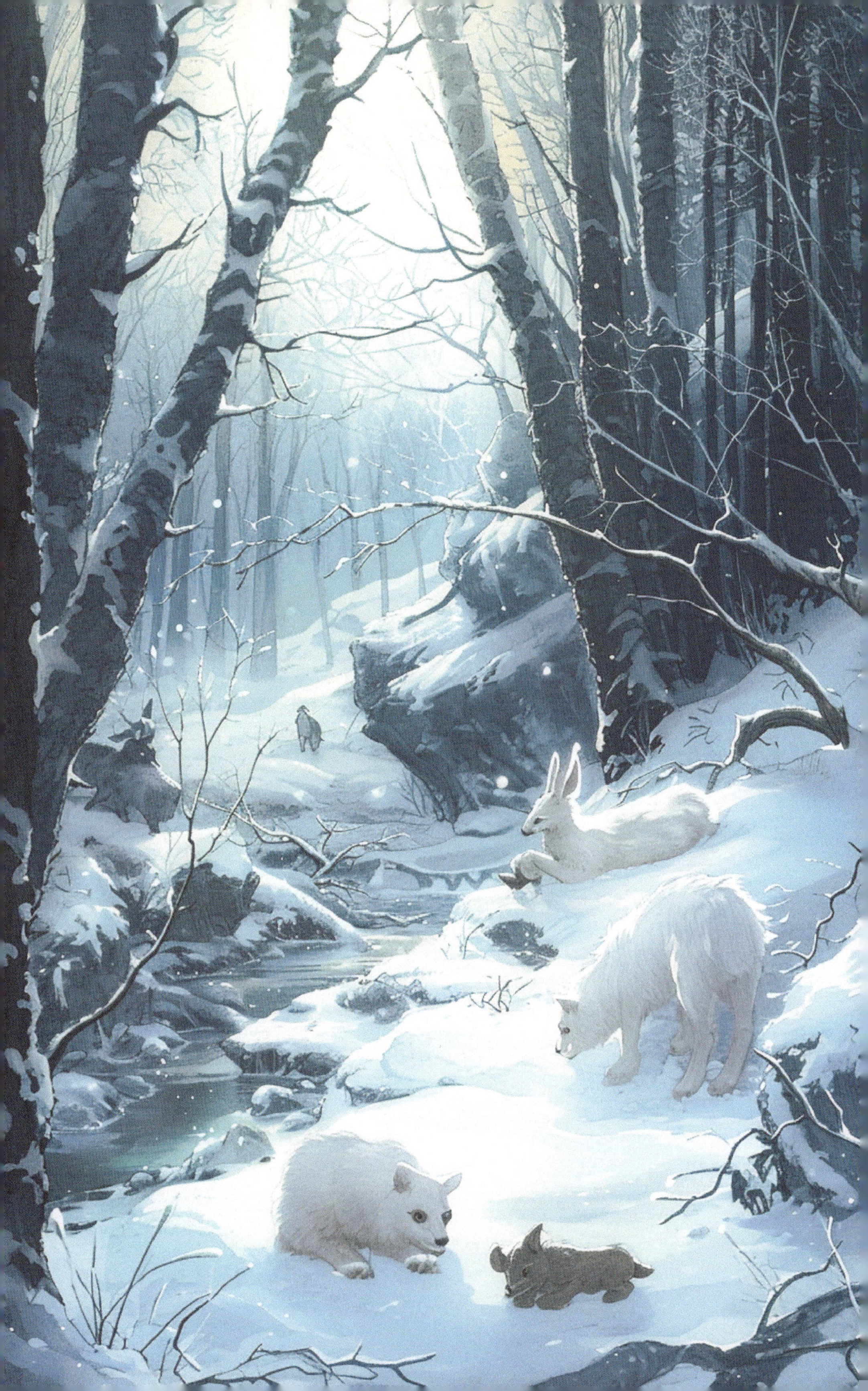

This is when Tao teaches us the power of stillness,
这是道教给我们寂静的力量的时候,

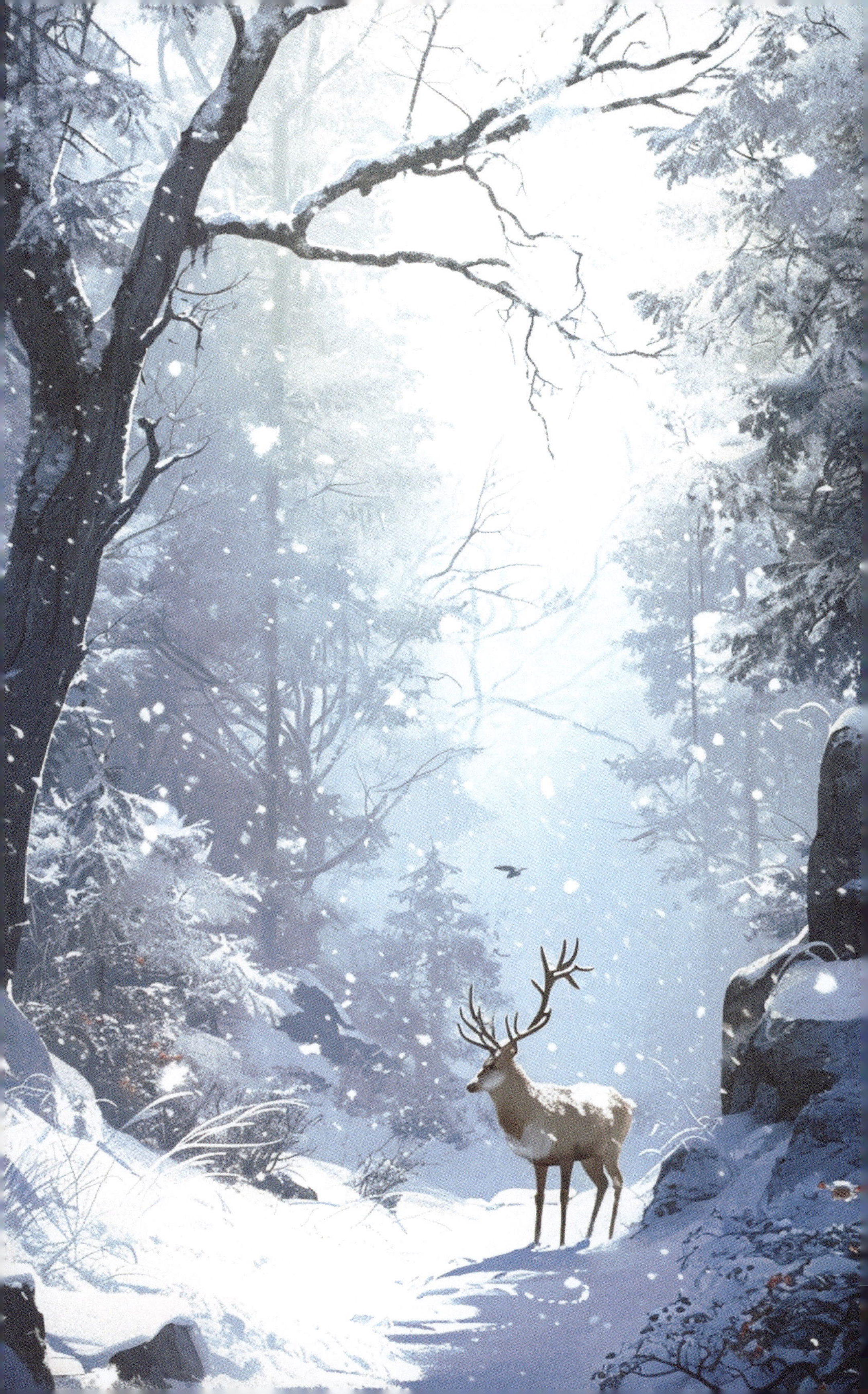

the strength found in quiet reflection."
在安静的反思中发现的力量。"

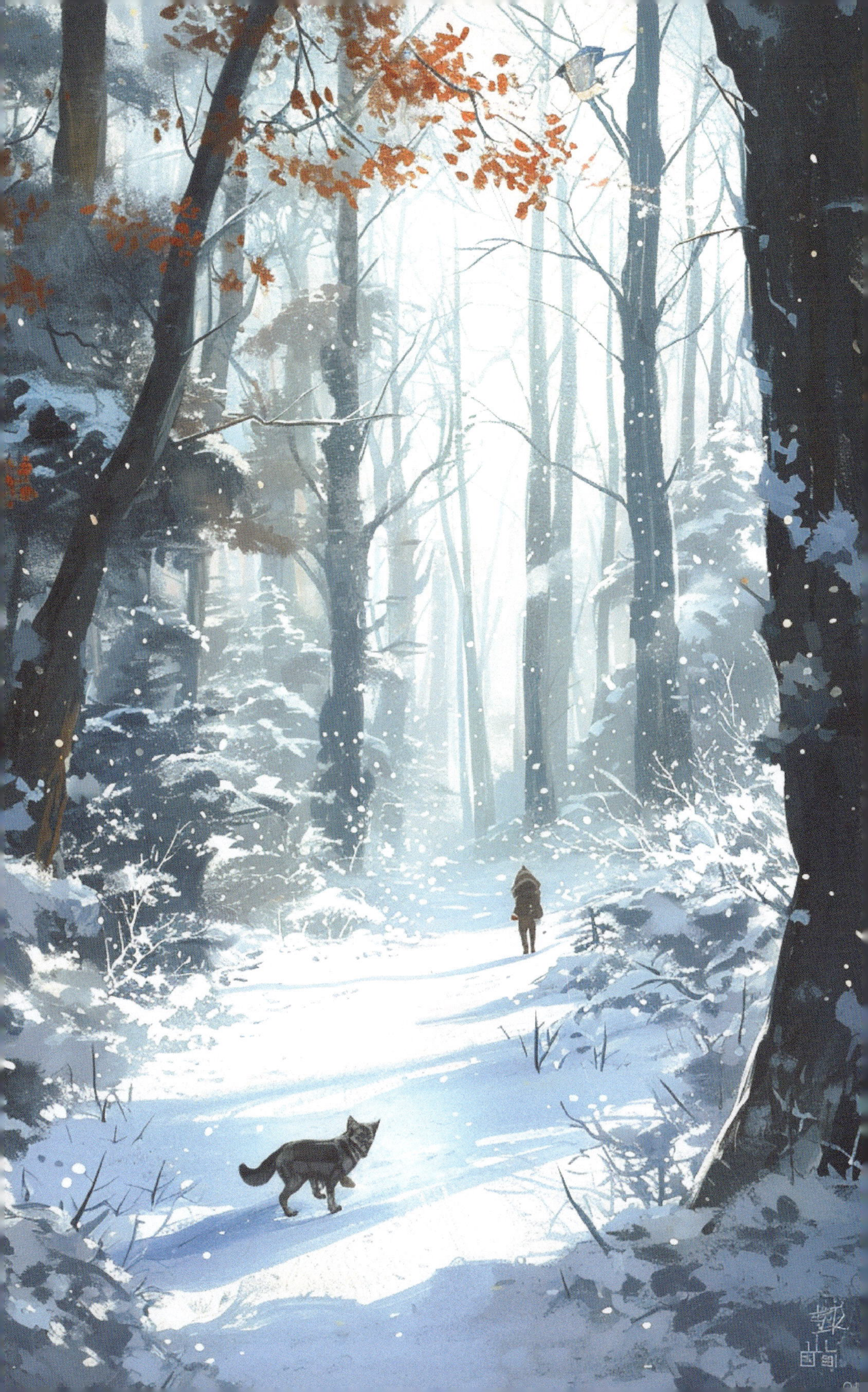

Yuki, a small snow leopard cub, curled up beside Master Ping.
雪豹小崽由纪蜷缩在平师傅身边。

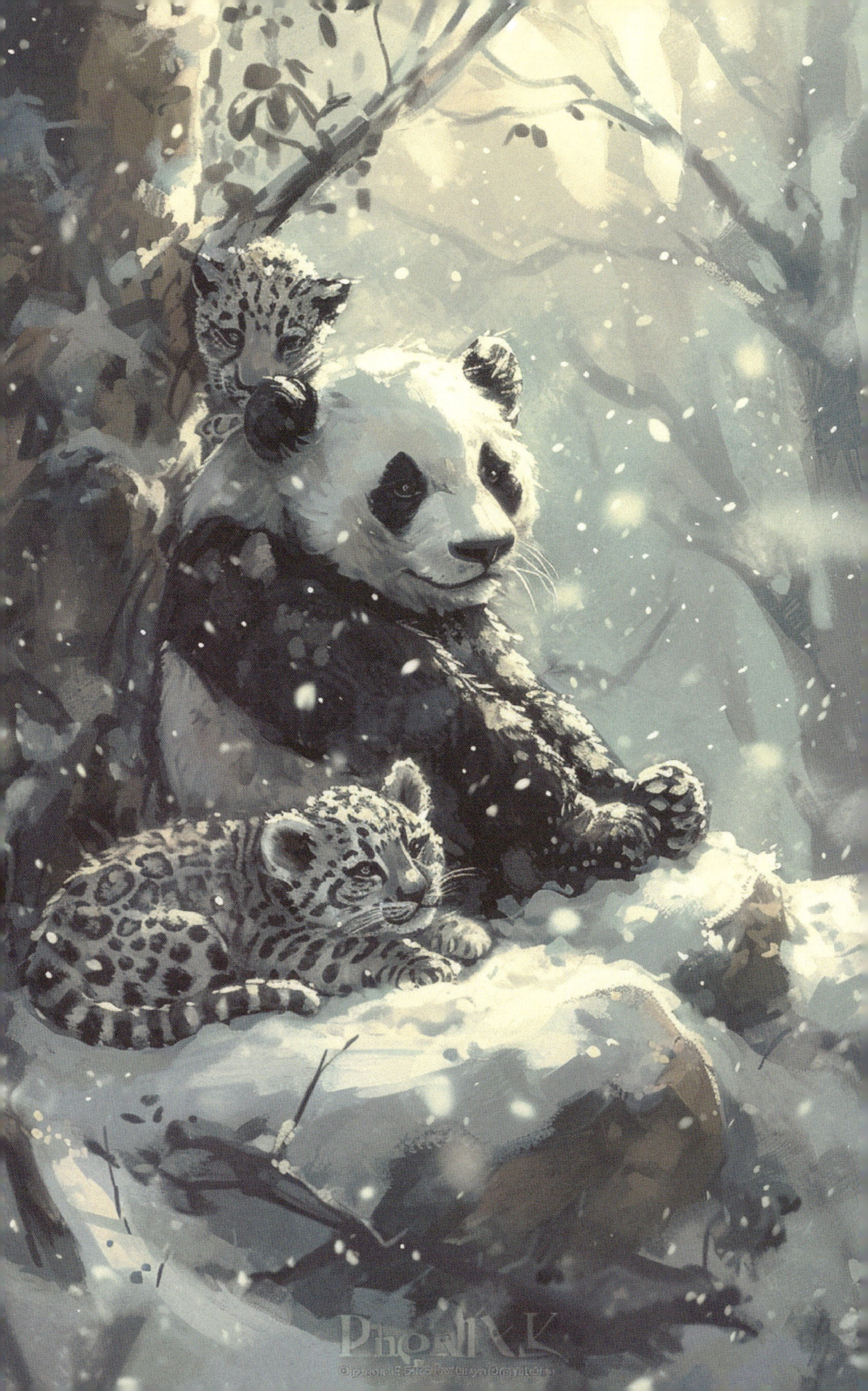

"Is Tao still here, even when everything is asleep?"
"即使一切都睡着了，道还在这里吗？"

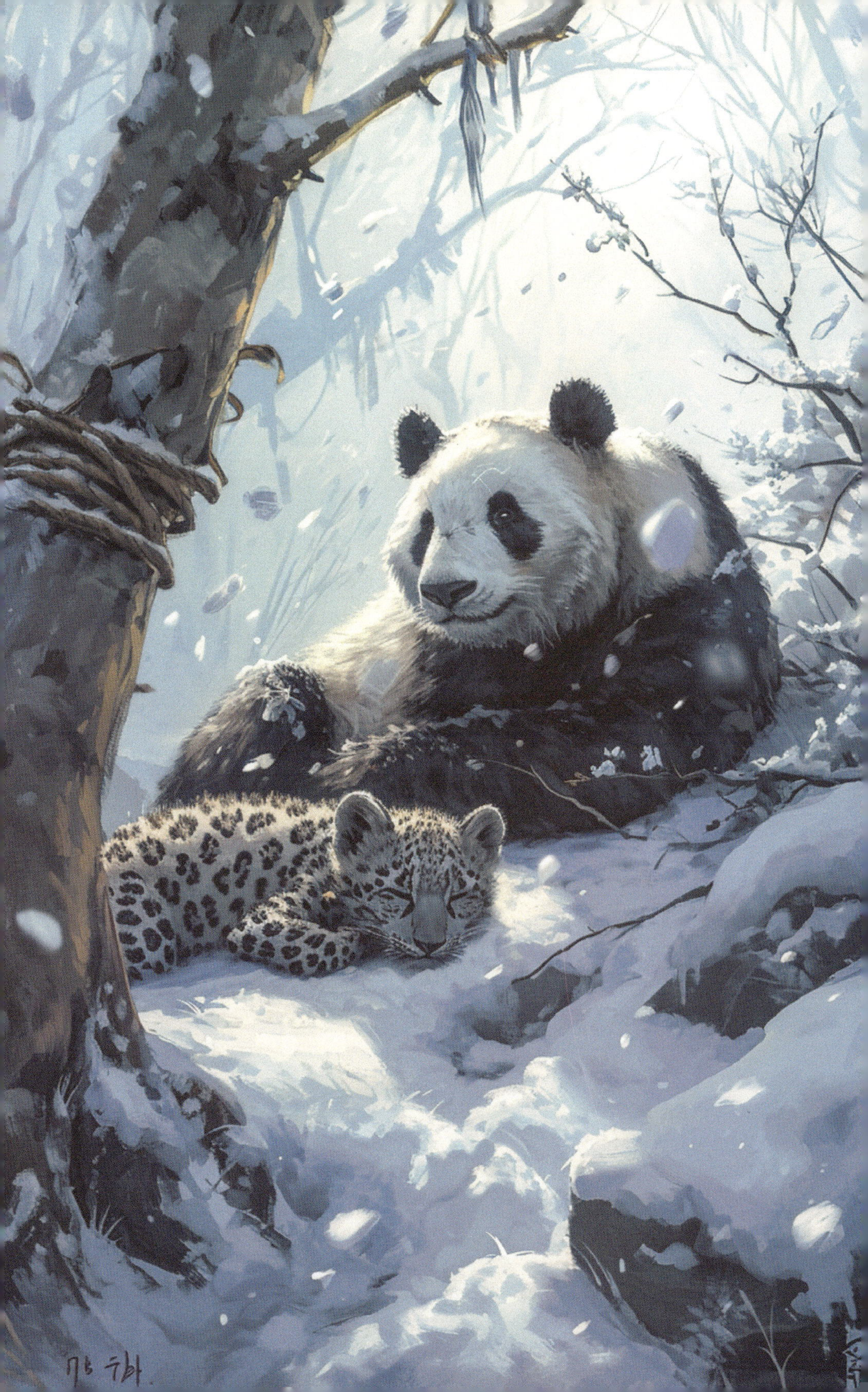

Master Ping nodded. "Yes, Yuki. Tao is always present,
平师傅点了点头。"是的，由纪。道一直都在，

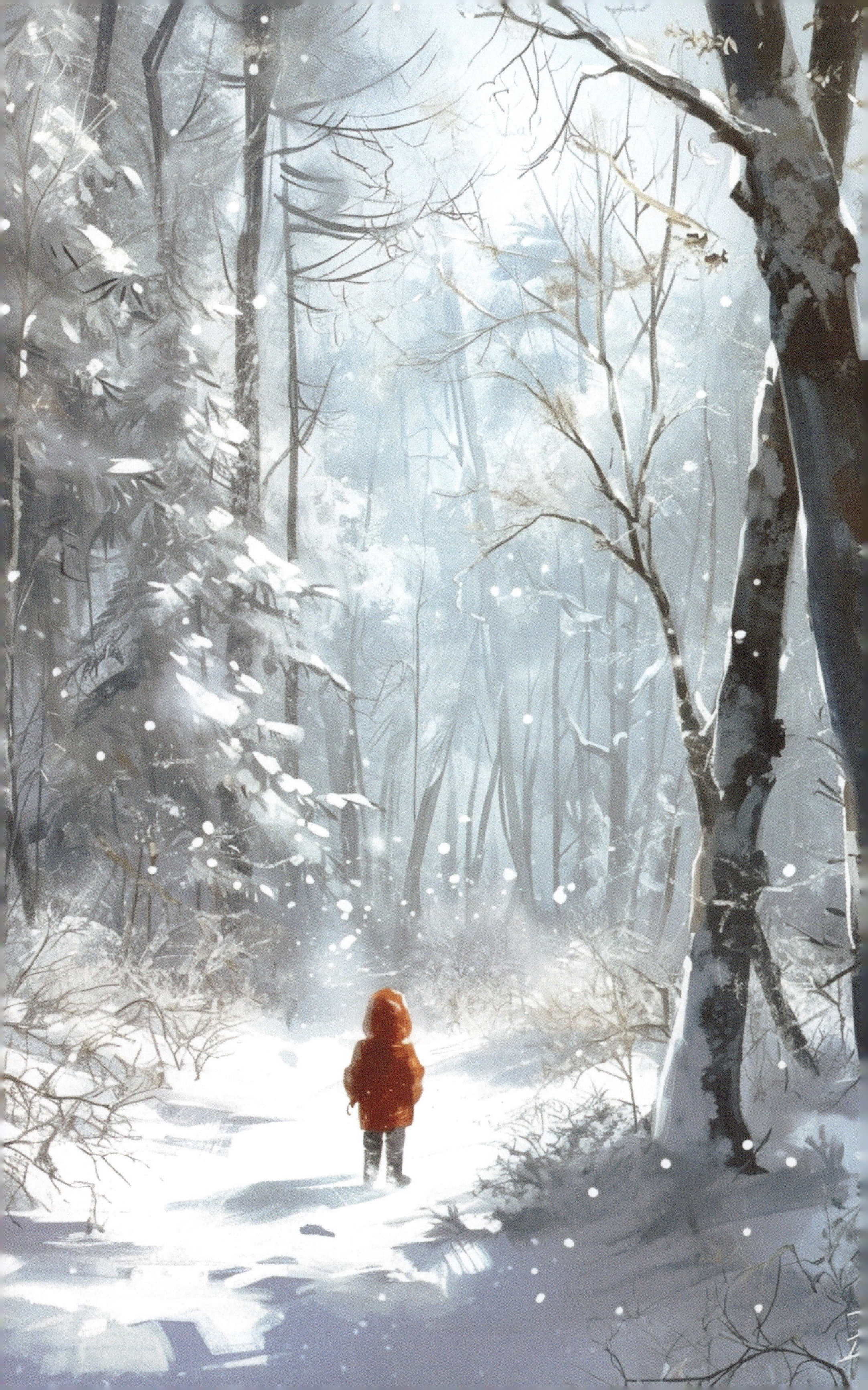

in the silence of the snow, in the peace of the winter night.
在雪的寂静中，在冬夜的宁静中。

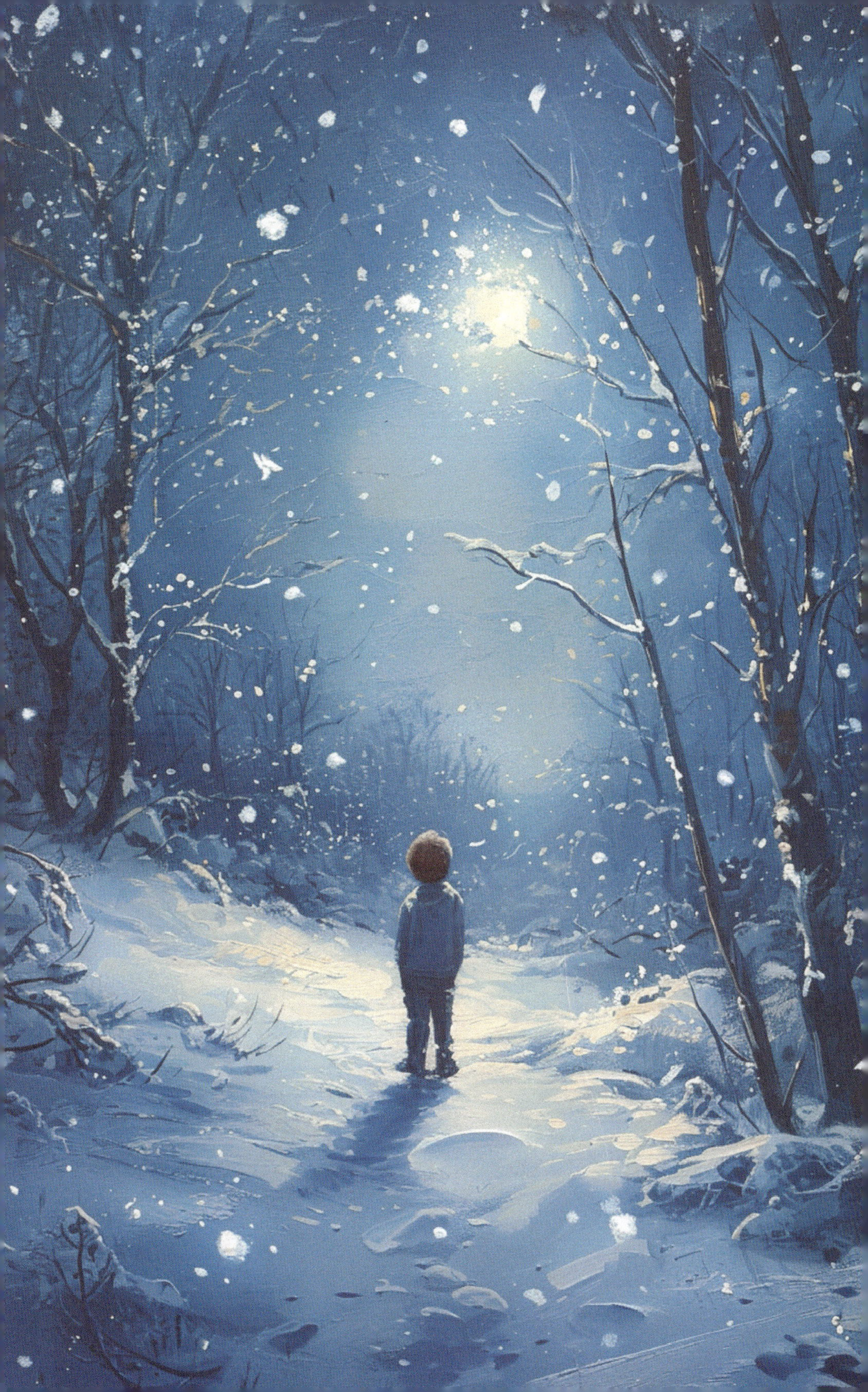

It is the rest before the new beginning."
这是新开始之前的休息."

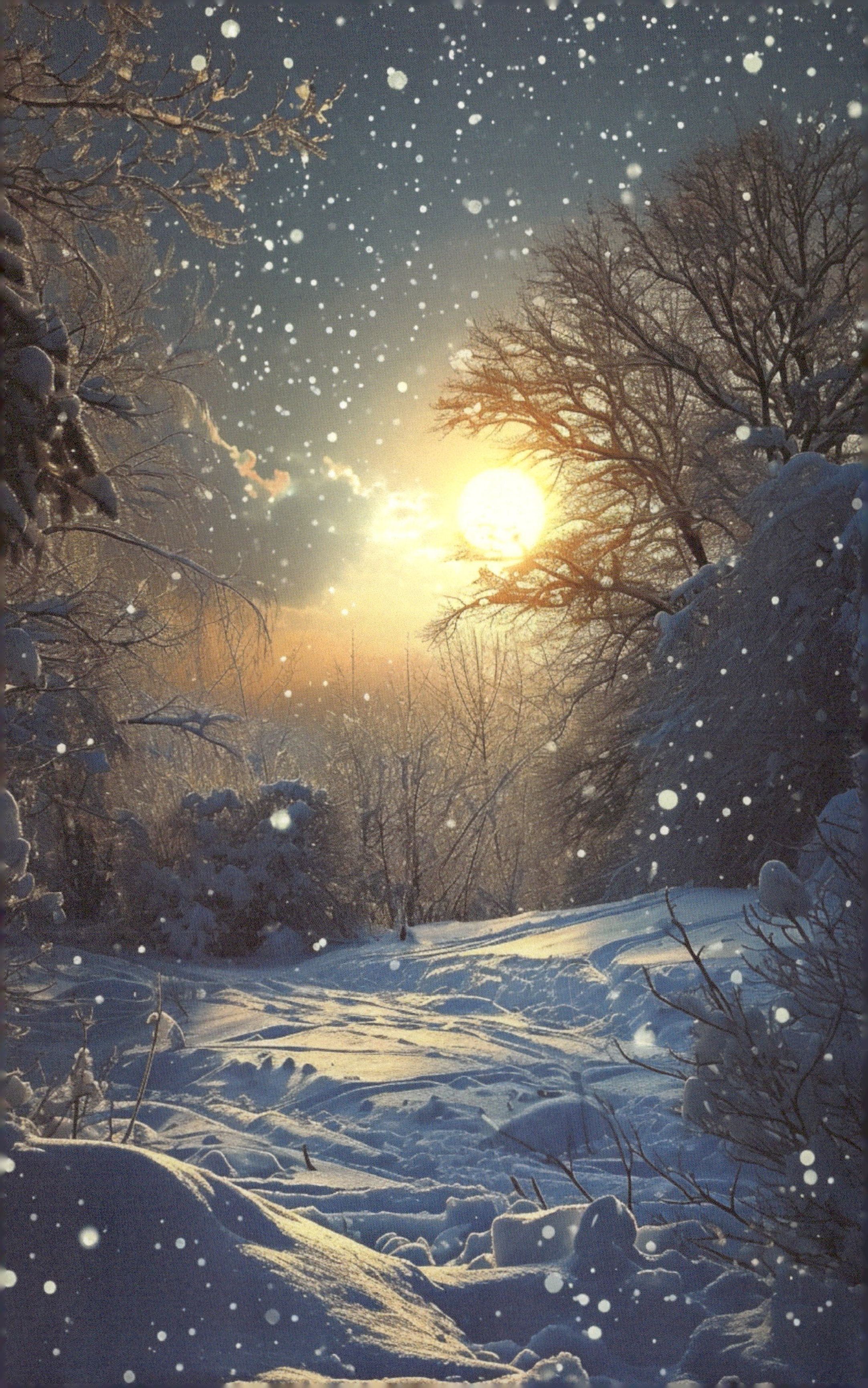

Chapter 5

-

The Circle of Tao

第五章

-

天道圆圆

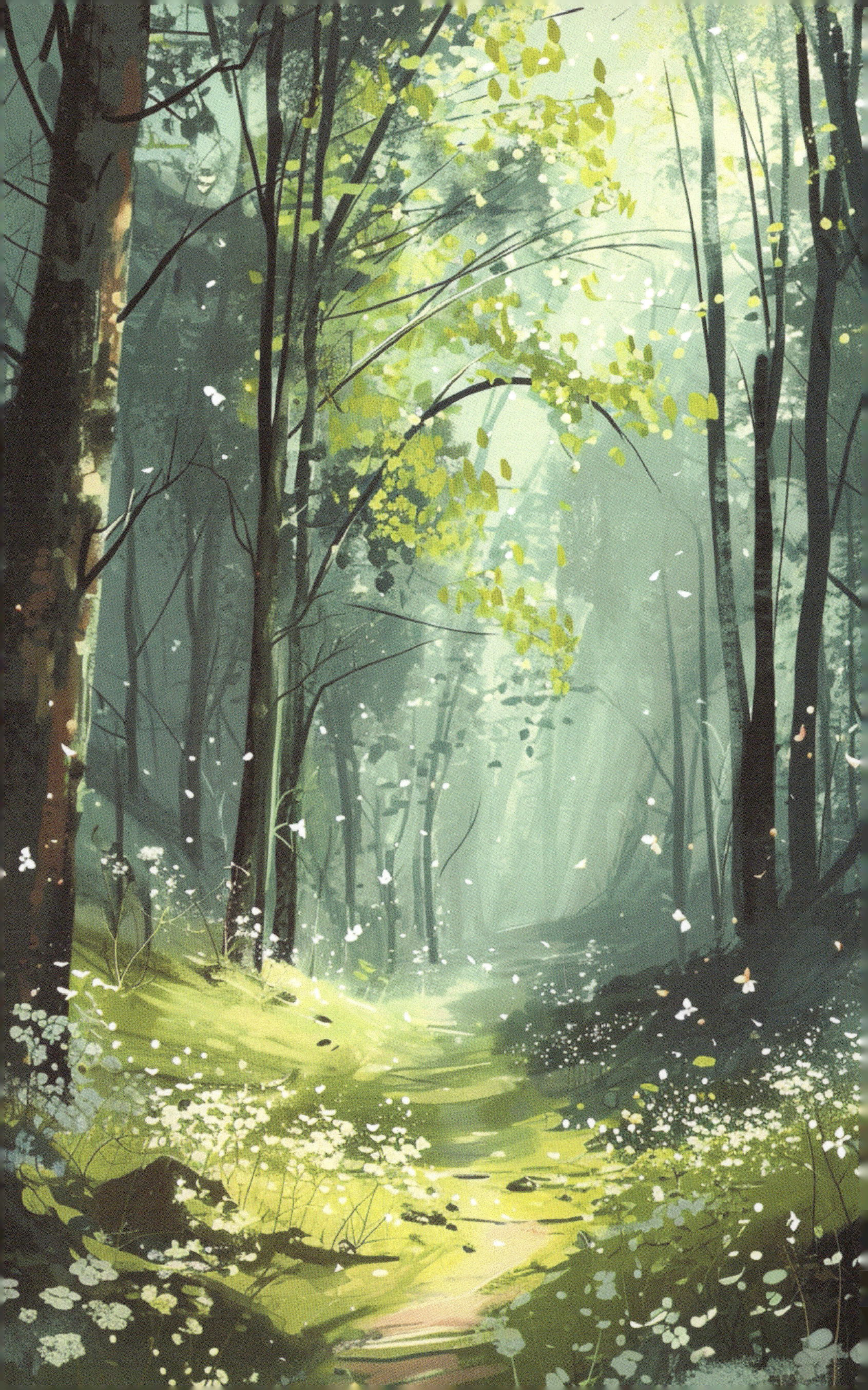

As the cycle of seasons came to a close,
随着季节循环的结束,

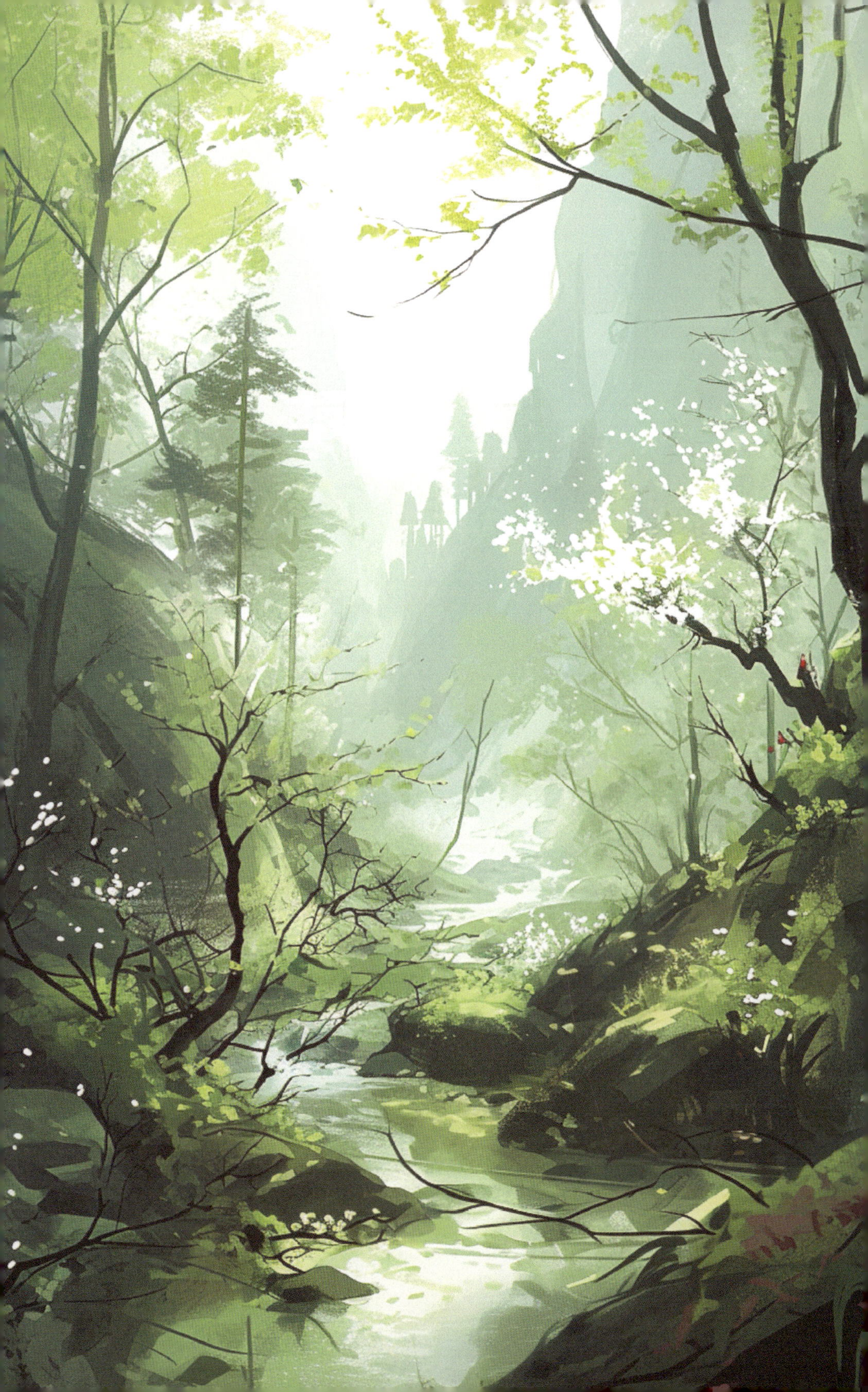

Master Ping gathered the animals once more.
平师傅再次召集了动物们。

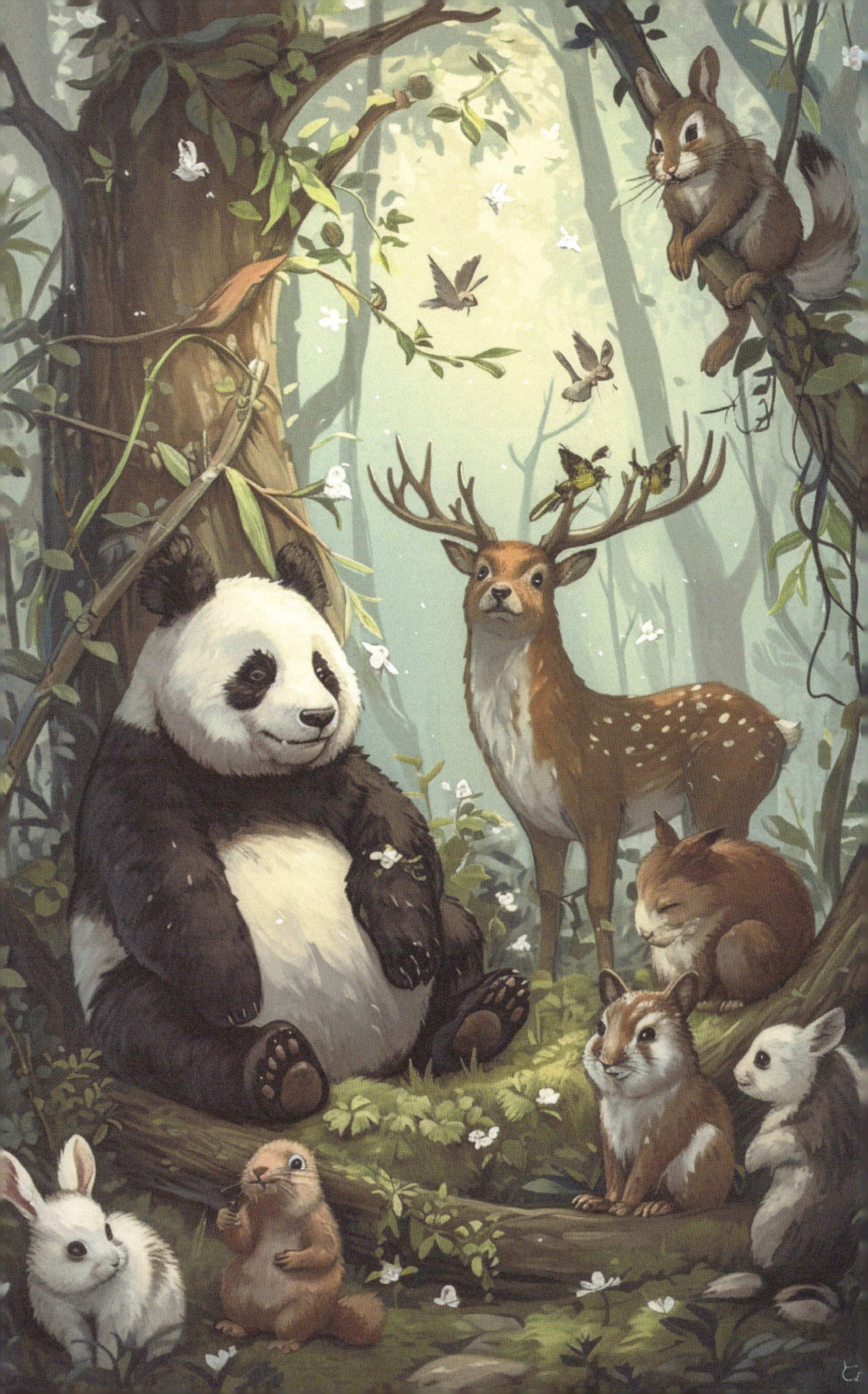

"The seasons are Tao's way of showing us the circle of life," he explained.

"季节是道向我们展示生命循环的方式，"他解释道。

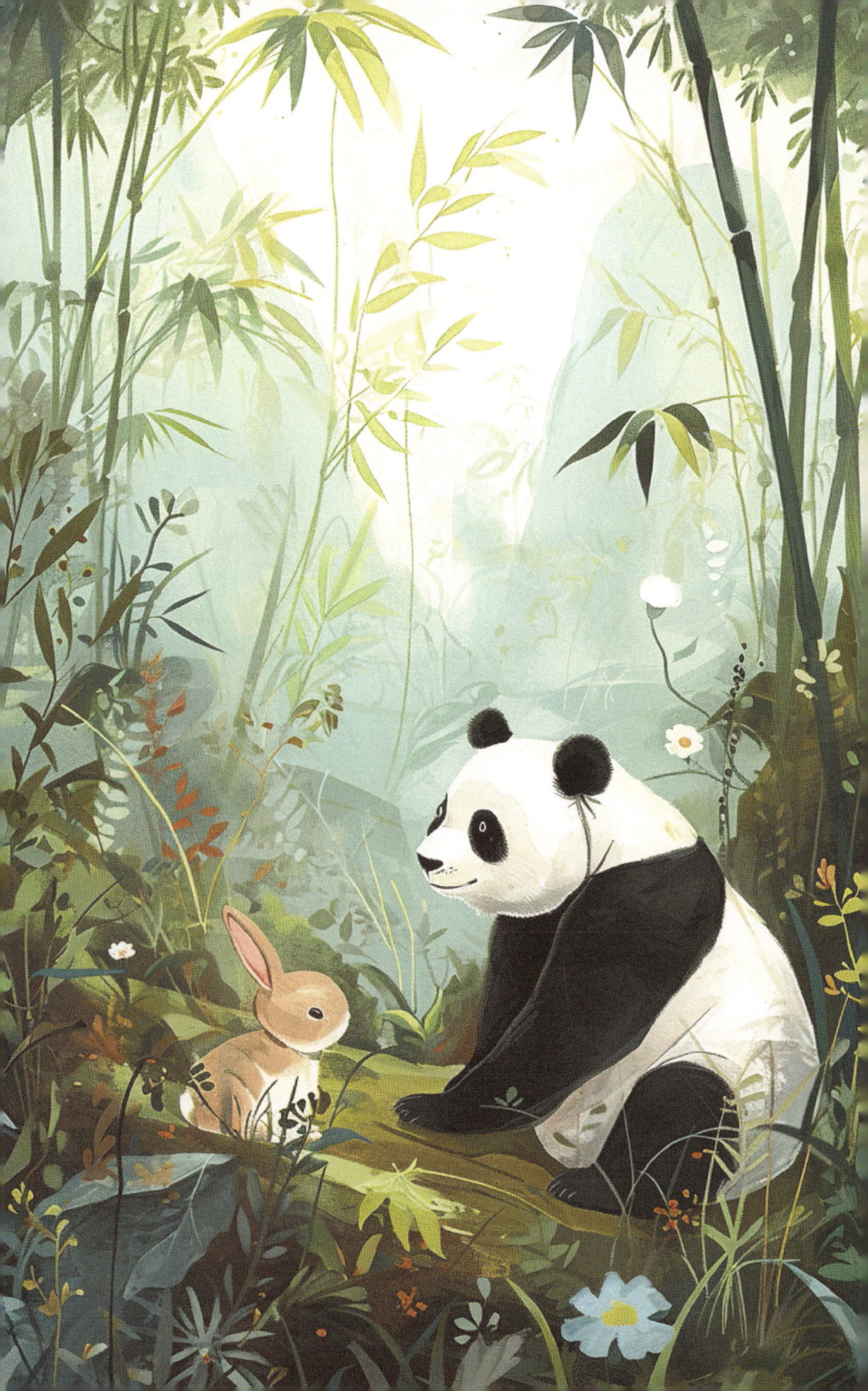

"Spring's beginnings, summer's growth, autumn's harvest, and winter's rest

"春生，夏长，秋收，冬藏

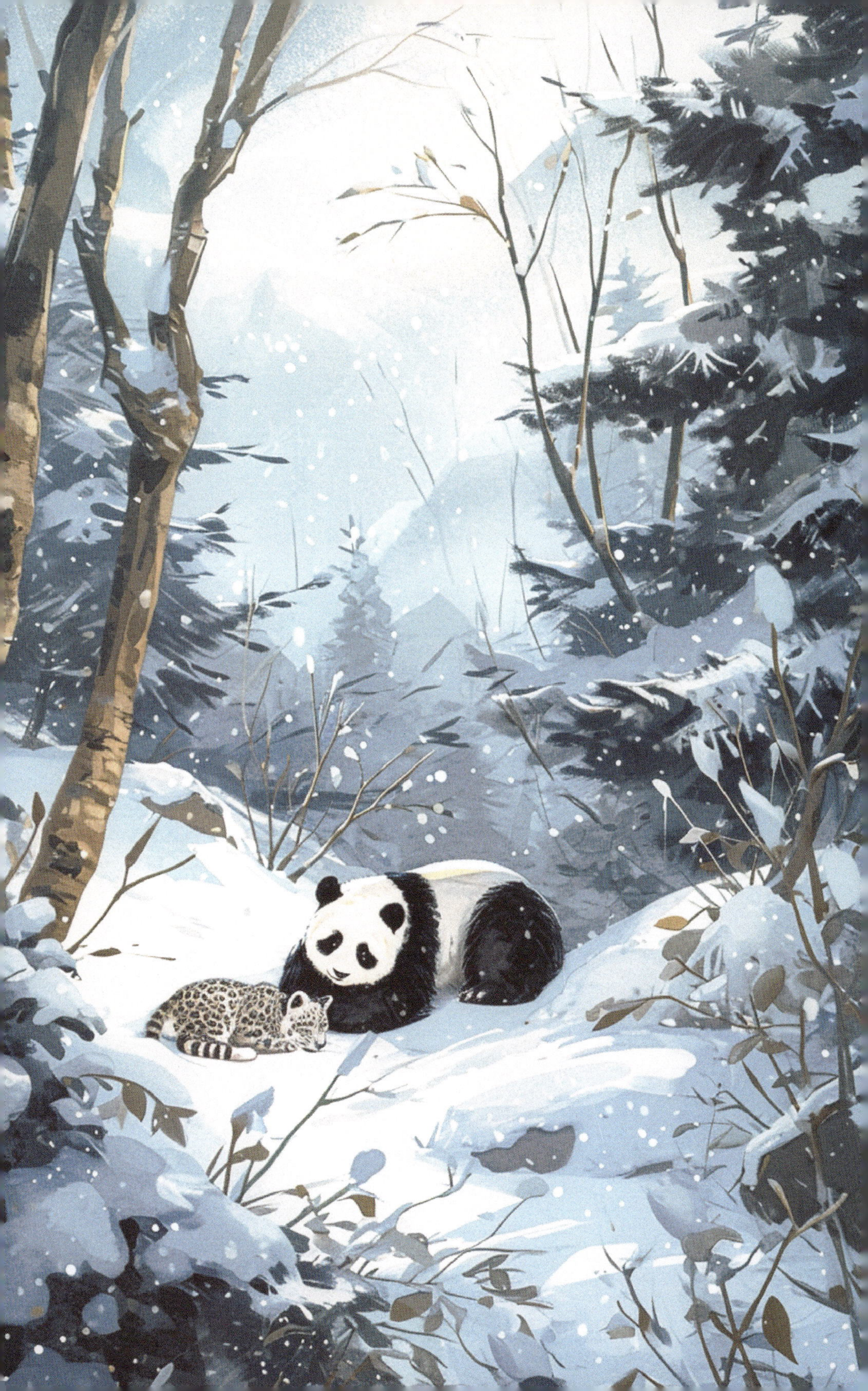

– all are parts of Tao's eternal dance."
– 所有这些都是道永恒之舞的一部分。"

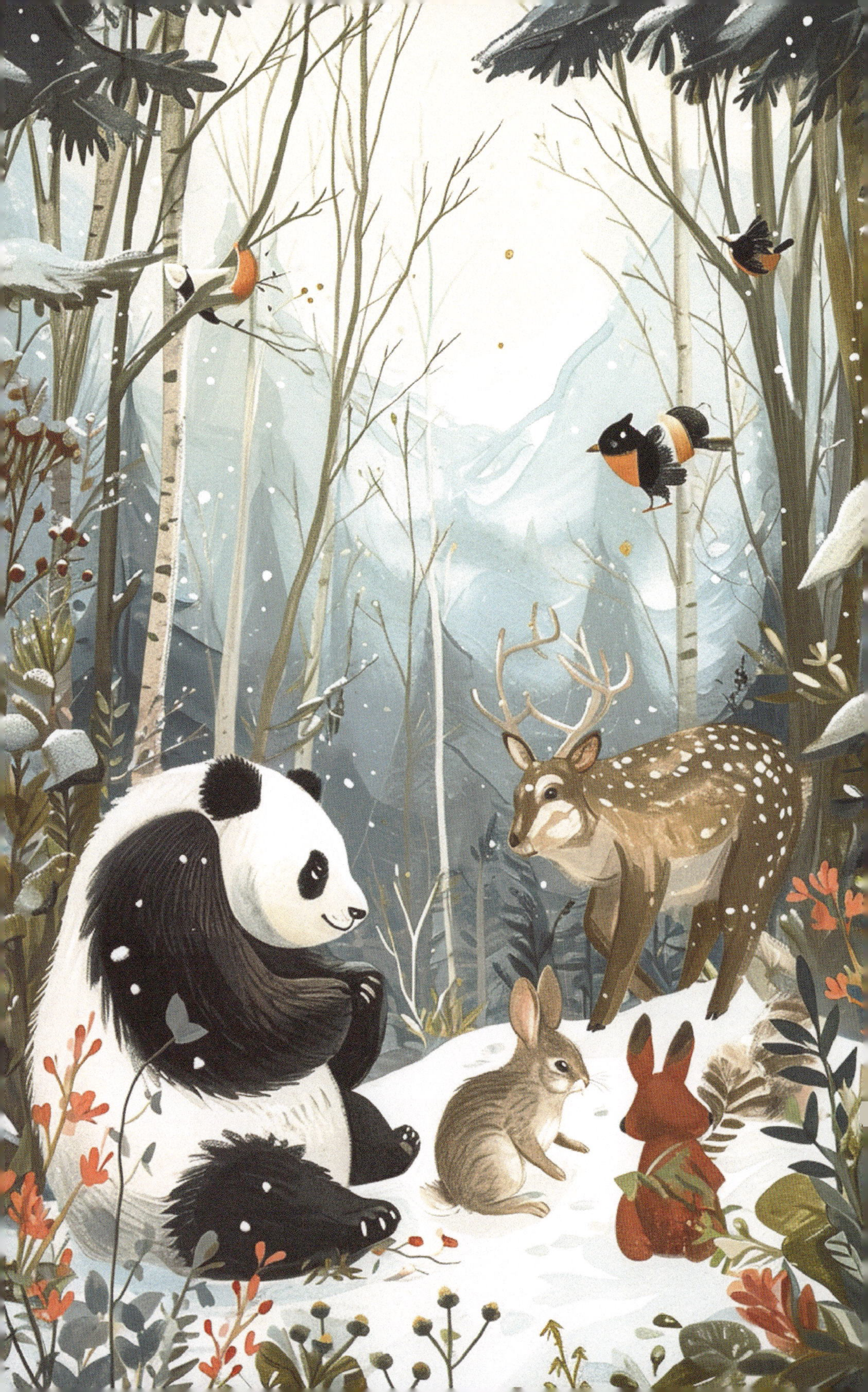

The animals sat in awe, their hearts filled with the wisdom of Tao.

动物们敬畏地坐着,他们的心中充满了道的智慧。

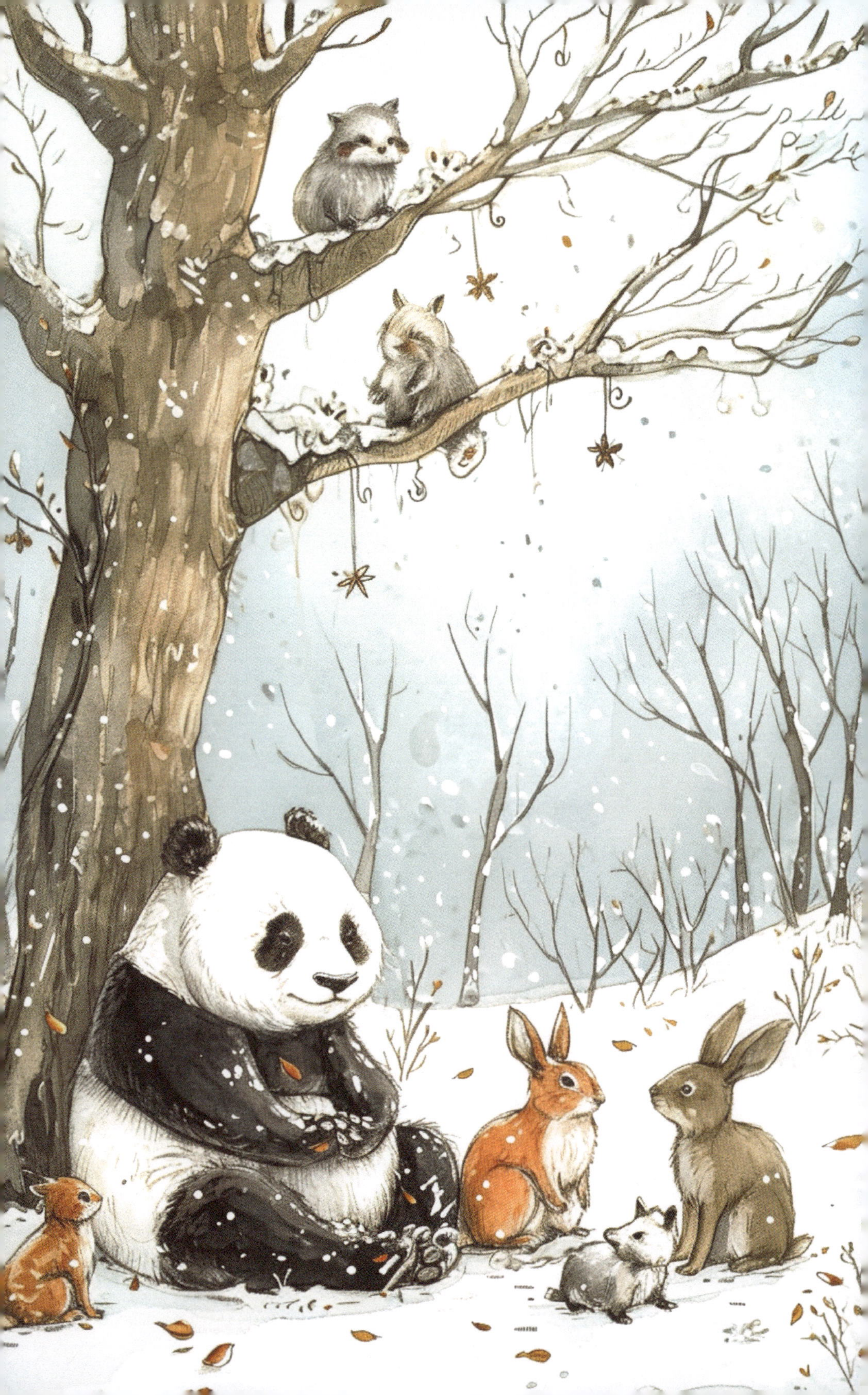

They understood that Tao was not just a force of nature but a guide for living,
他们明白，道不仅是一种自然的力量，而且是生活的向导，

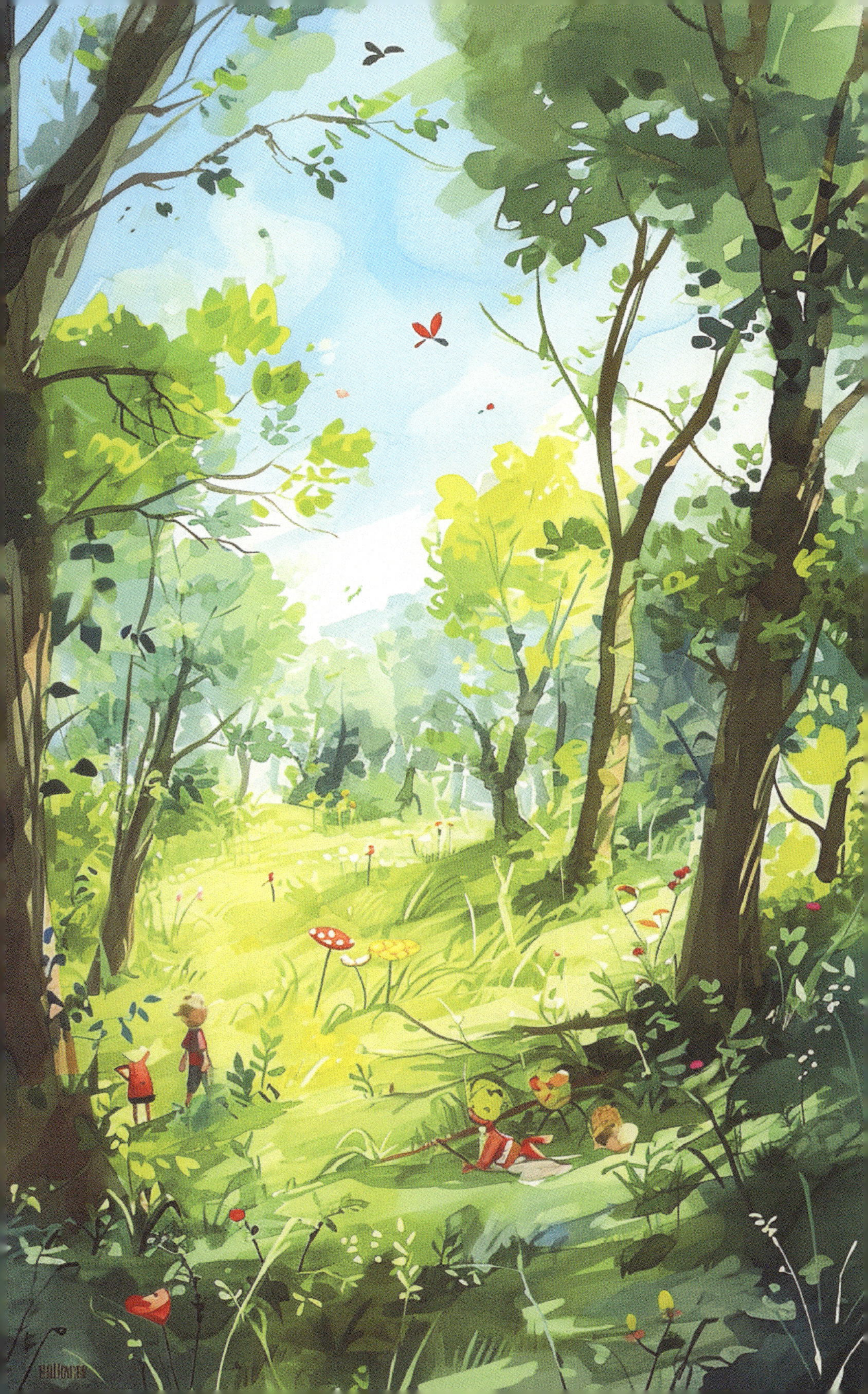

a path to harmony and balance.
一条通往和谐与平衡的道路。

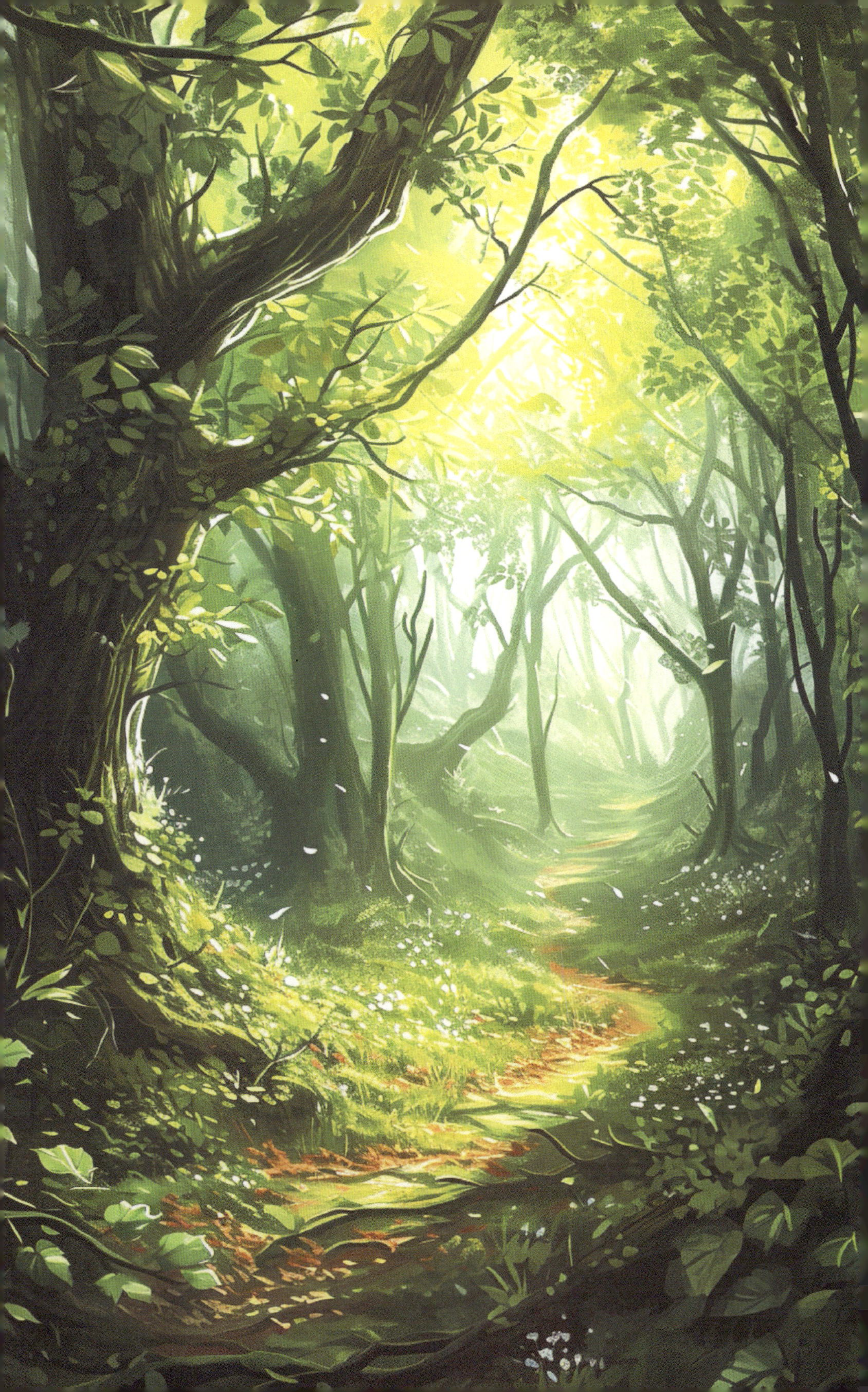

"Remember, my young friends," Master Ping said,
"记住，我的年轻朋友们，"平师傅说，

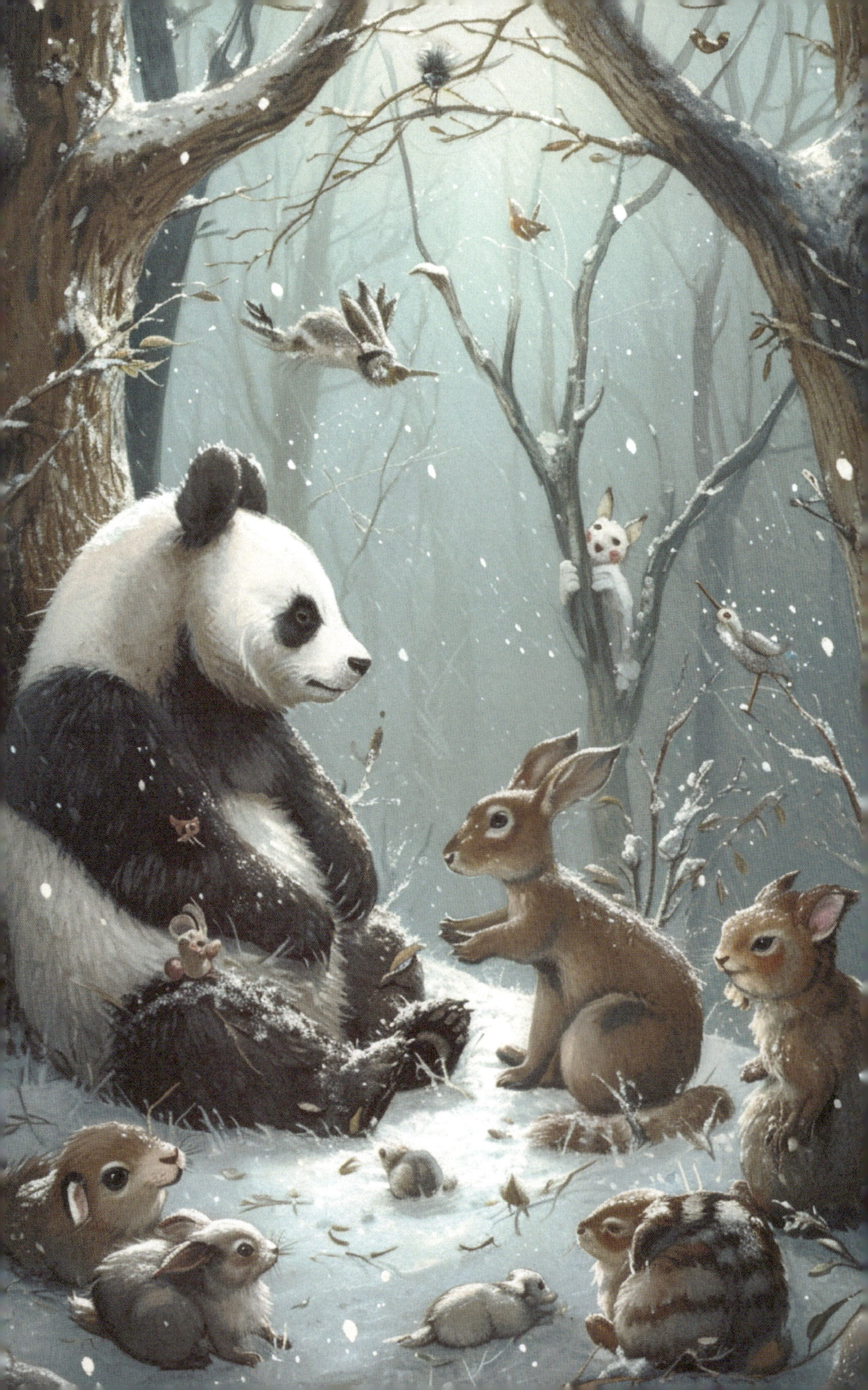

"Tao is in everything and everyone.
"道存在于一切事物和每个人中。

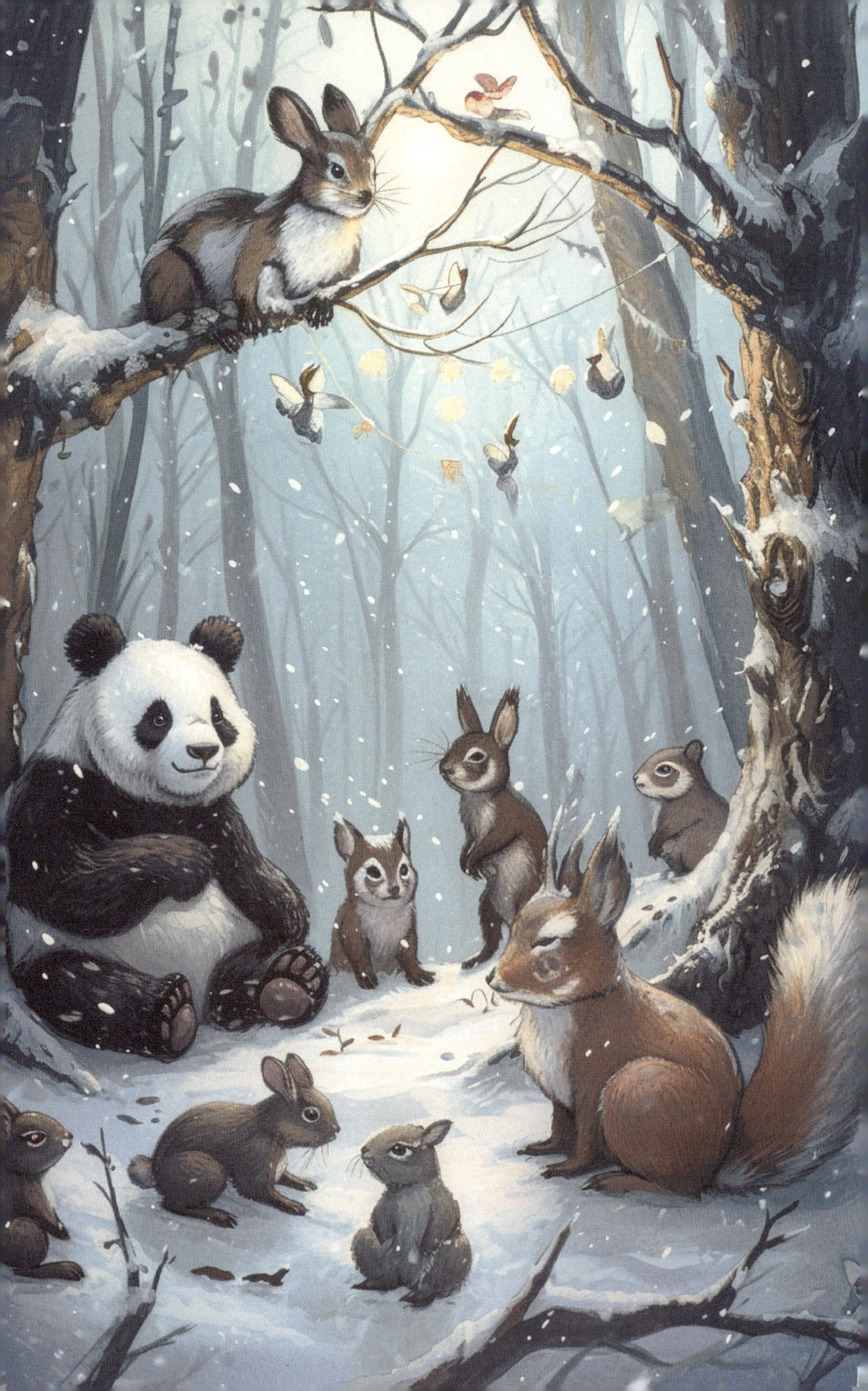

It is the unseen energy that connects us all,
它是连接我们所有人的看不见的能量，

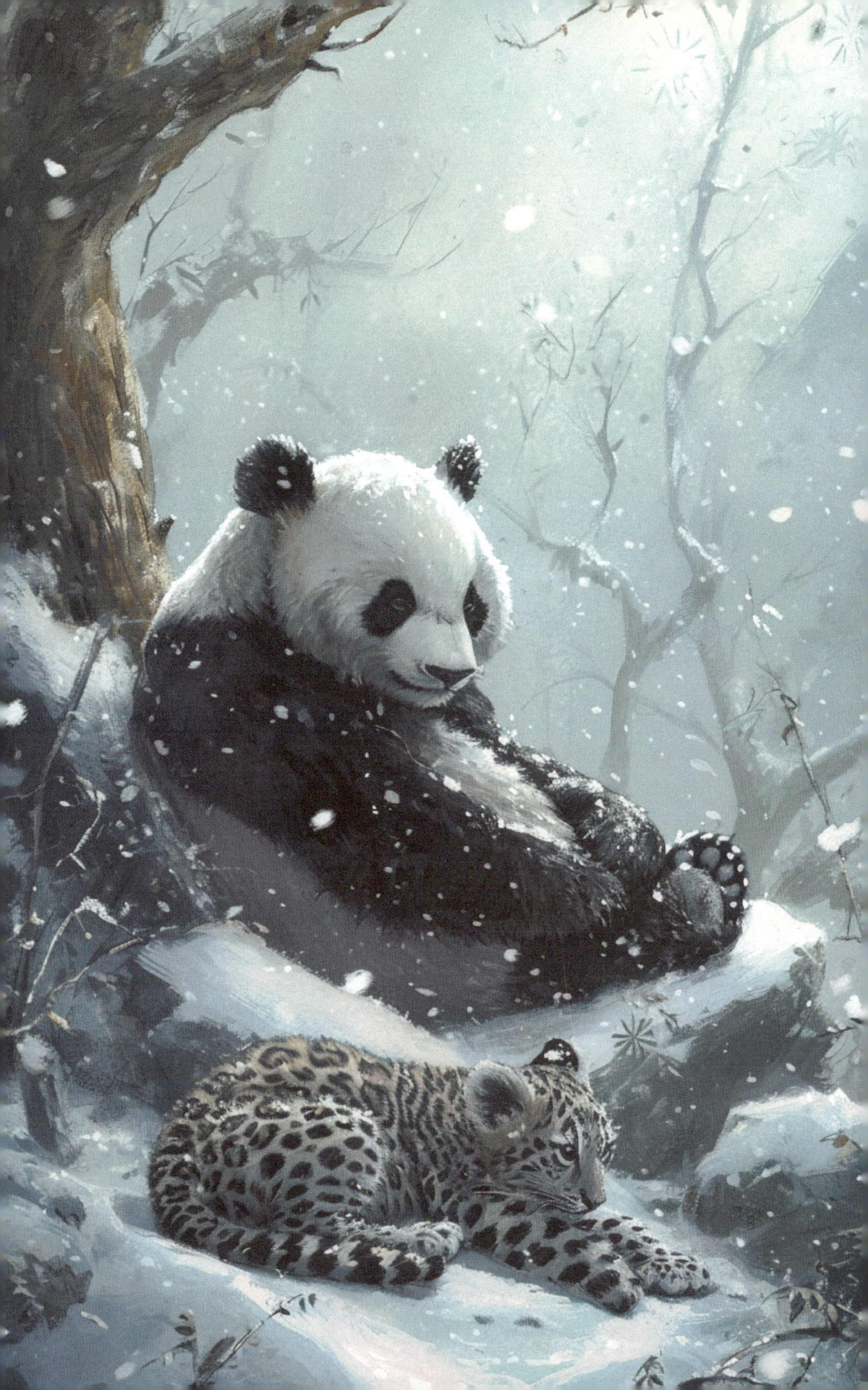

the eternal rhythm of the universe."
宇宙永恒的节奏。"

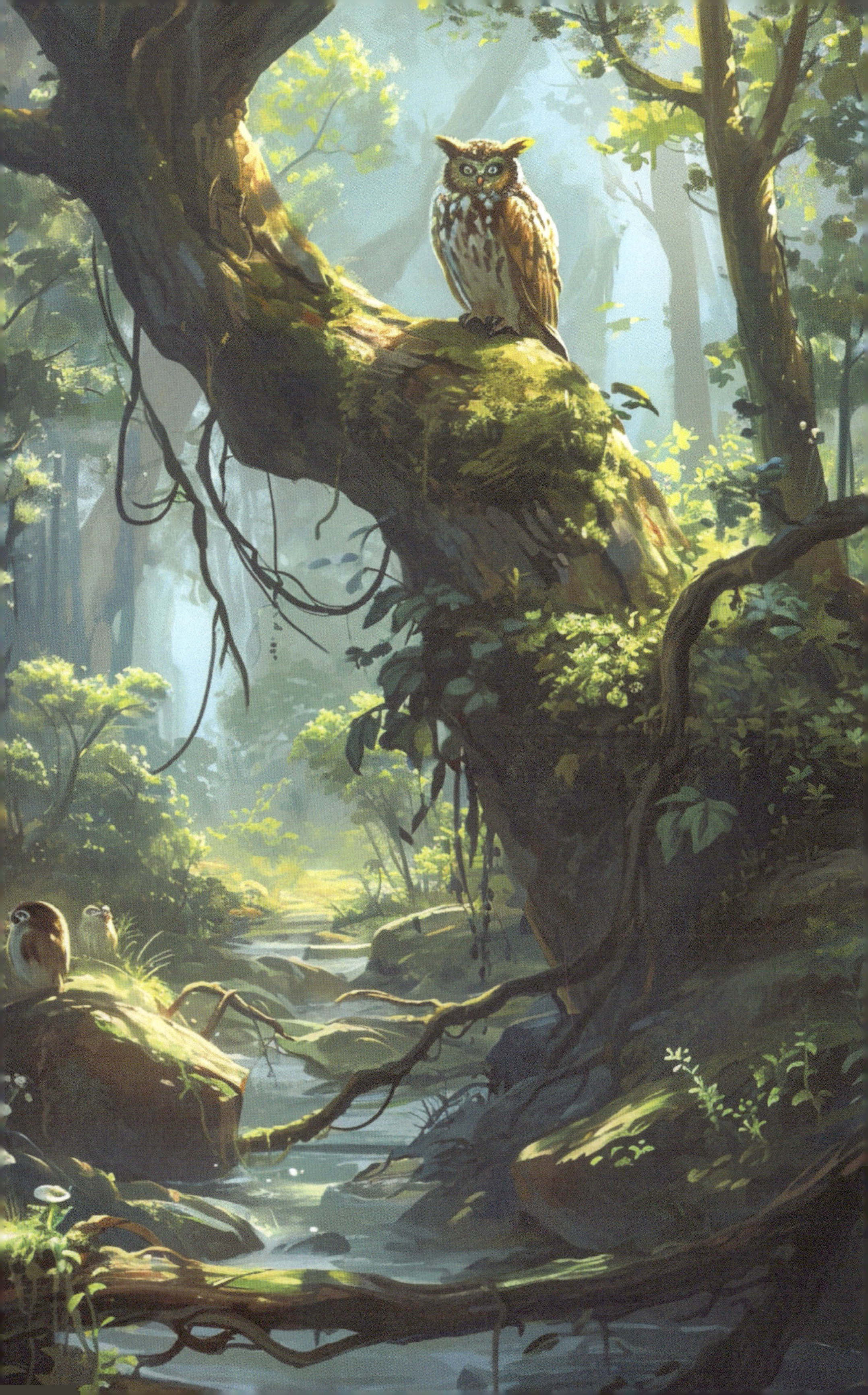

As the animals dispersed,
随着动物们的散去，

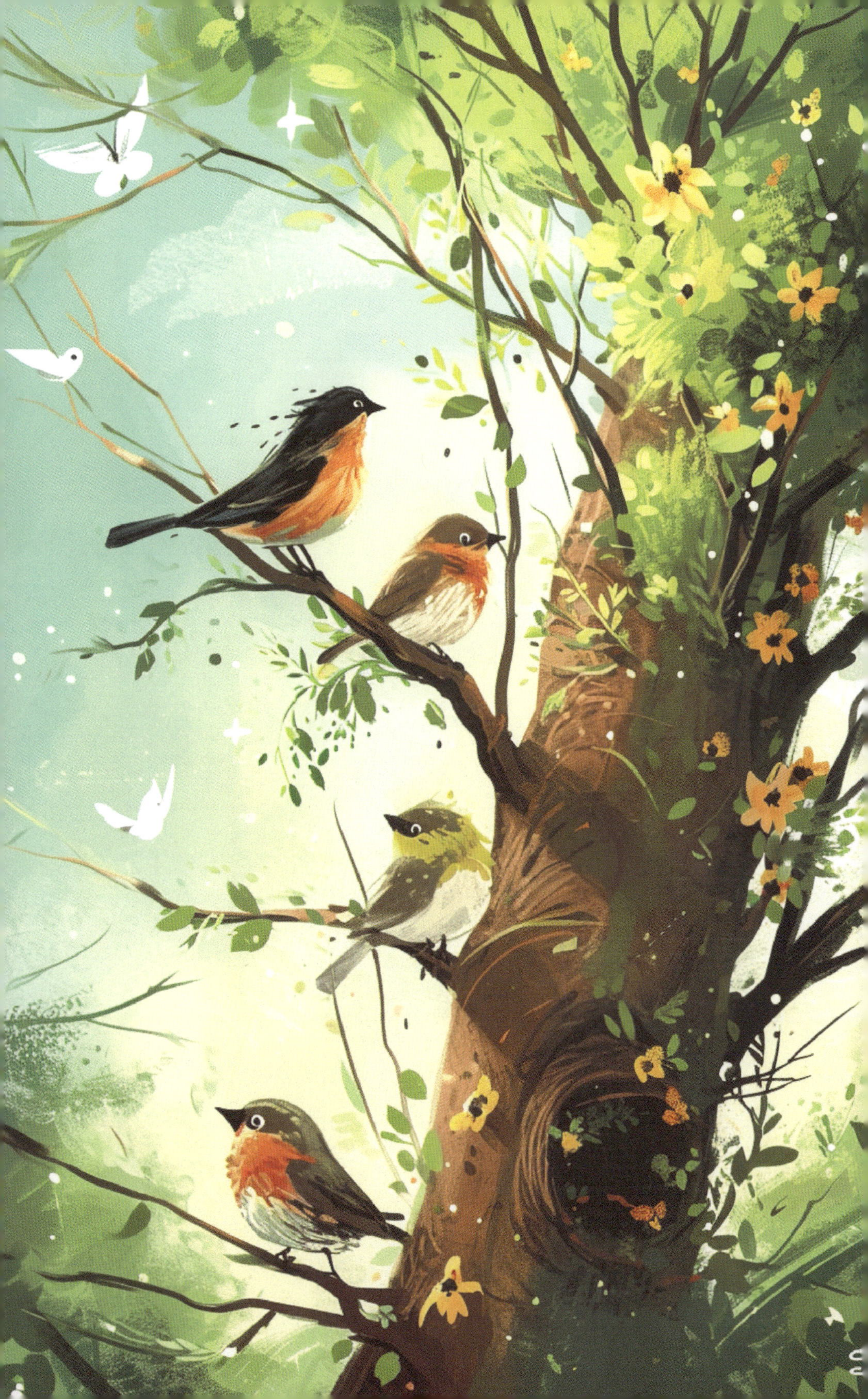

each carried with them the lessons of Tao
每个都带着道的知识

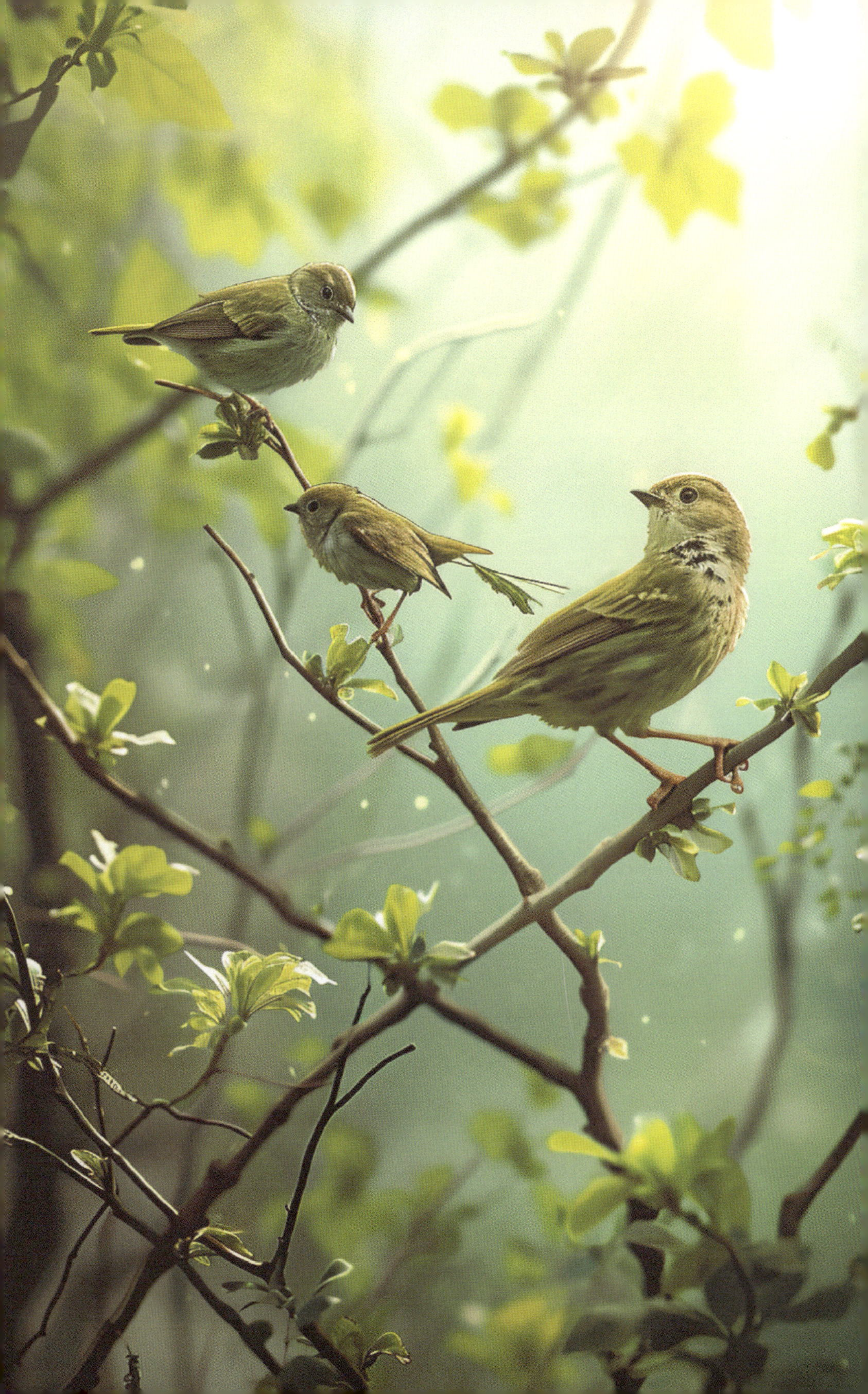

– lessons of growth, balance, stillness, and the eternal cycle of life.
– 成长、平衡、静止和生命永恒循环的教训。

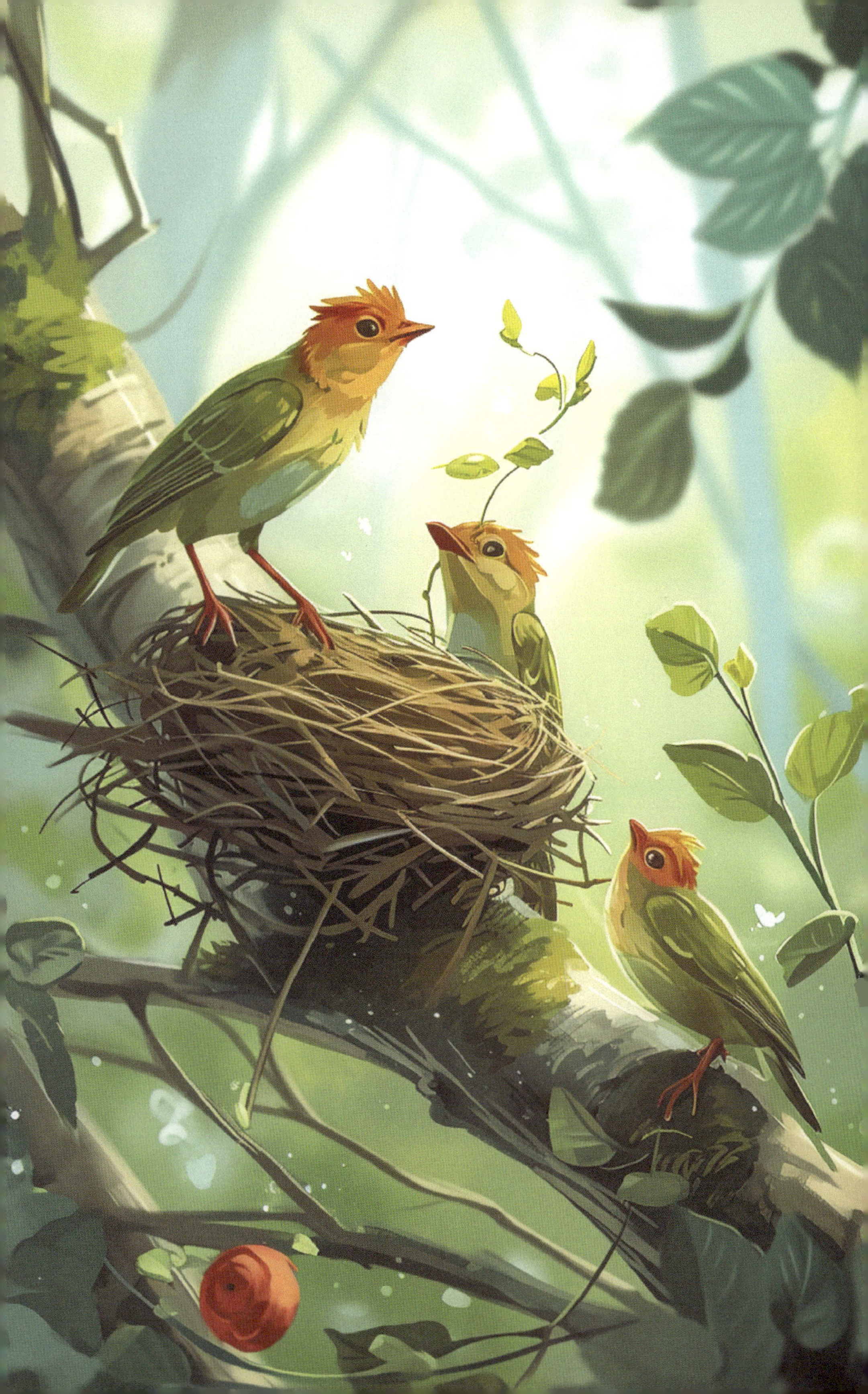

**In the heart of the mystical forest,
在神秘森林的中心，**

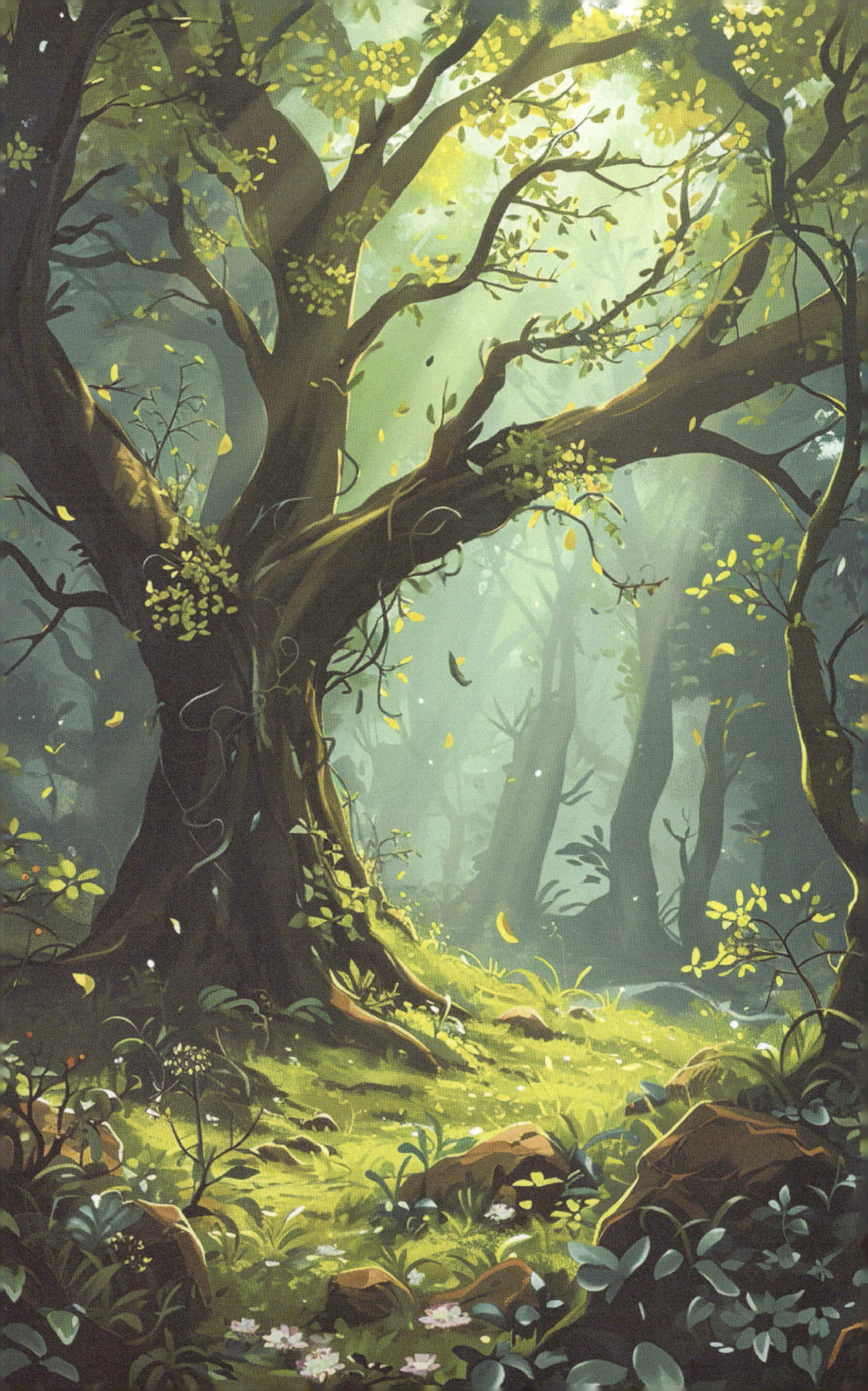

the wisdom of Tao
continued to flow,
道的智慧不斷流淌，

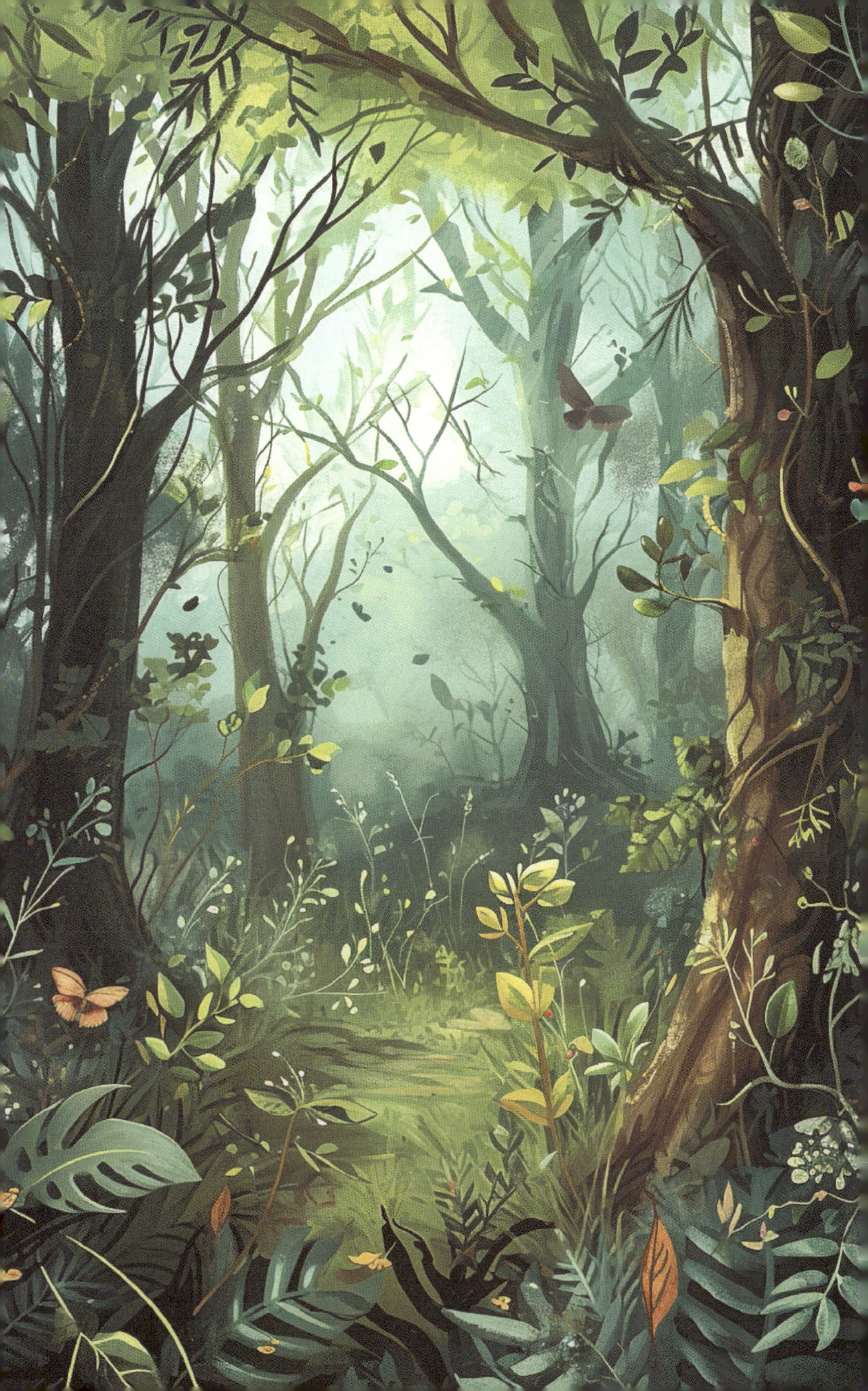

timeless and ever-present.
不朽而永恒。

Printed in Great Britain
by Amazon